The Renegade Writer's
Query
Letters
that Rock

The Renegade Writer's Query Letters that Rock

By Linda Formichelli and Diana Burrell

Marion Street Press, Inc.
Oak Park, Illinois

Like this book?

Then you'll love...

The Renegade Writer: A Totally Unconventional Guide to Freelance Writing Success (ISBN 19333380-0-8, Marion Street Press, Inc.)

The Renegade Writer blog at www.therenegadewriter.com

and Linda Formichelli's e-course on freelance writing at www.lindaformichelli.com

Cover design by Anne Locascio

ISBN 1-933338-09-1

Printed in U.S.A.
Printing 10 9 8 7 6 5 4 3 2 1

Marion Street Press, Inc.
PO Box 2249
Oak Park, IL 60303
866-443-7987
www.marionstreetpress.com

Section I: Query Letter Q&A

Section II: Query Letters That Rock!

Introduction

One day as we were ~~gossiping~~ talking business over some coffee (Diana's) and hot chocolate (Linda's) we mused aloud how fun it would be to tail an editor for a day. You know, hang out with her in the office, pore through the queries that ended up in her inbox, and help her shoot down hideous story ideas. Well, after 30 seconds of musing, we figured out we'd have to wear skirts and maybe even pantyhose and makeup. And frankly, we're not the sadistic types who get off on breaking writers' hearts. We went back to the important work before us: How could we show — not tell — writers what works in a query letter versus what doesn't?

Like many people, Diana learns best by watching how others do things. For example, she loves to cook. From the time she could hold a wooden spoon, she stood at the wood-block counter in her grandmother's Vermont kitchen and watched how an expert creamed butter and sugar together, beating them till they were light and fluffy enough to produce meltingly tender cookies and cakes. When she was older, she asked a butcher to show her how to butterfly a chicken. She learned how to flambé by watching Julia Child on Saturday afternoons on PBS. If you want to be successful, watch the successful. Then copy everything they do.

Suddenly, it hit her. Why not give readers a chance to get a behind-the-scenes story on a query letter — and ask editors to explain exactly what they loved about the letter? We gave each other a high five and Diana shot the book idea off to Ed Avis at Marion Street Press, who...

Okay, we have to be honest. He rejected it. We don't need to go into details why, since it's obvious Ed since had an epiphany. That, or maybe the three goons we sent over to his office knocked some sense into him. But as he told us later, "I couldn't stop thinking about the idea." Sometimes a crack to the ol' noggin can do that to a person. A more likely explanation is that a good idea isn't always so obvious at first glance, but like wine or Pierce Brosnan, it gets better with time.

After Ed called us to say, "Onward Renegades!" we picked ourselves off the floor, dusted ourselves off, and then said, "Oh no! Now we have get editors to talk to us!" We put this off as long as we could, figuring that when these editors heard us banging on their doors, they'd ignore us and pretend they were actually working. Lo and behold, nearly every editor we approached was happy to dish. We asked them if they'd be willing to share a query letter that rocked their world and tell us exactly what they loved about it. Some of them struggled to find a good query letter (I know, that depressed us too), yet others had more than one show-stopper tucked in their files. We then contacted the writers, buttering them up by telling them how much the editor had loved their queries, and most of them gladly shared their work and thought processes with us.

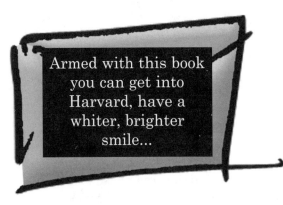

Armed with this book you can get into Harvard, have a whiter, brighter smile...

Our aim was to get a good variety of magazines in this book: everything from newsstand favorites to pubs with a very limited distribution. Some magazines pay $2 per word and up ... others pay only 20 cents per word (but they all do pay writers). We also tried to cover all levels of experience. Writers who have little freelancing experience wrote some of the letters in this book. (One writer

Introduction

admitted to us he didn't really know much about writing query letters — in fact, he'd never read a book about freelancing.) Other writers here have dozens of credits, or even have contributing editor status. Whether you're a beginning freelancer or an experienced pro, we think you'll find all these letters helpful. You'll get a birds-eye view on how an editor thinks, and you'll also see that wildly different letters have commonalties: the writer tends to have a voice and style that appeals to the magazine, and the stories themselves are engaging, well-researched, and worth the magazine's investment.

We both teach writing courses, and we get a lot of great questions from our students about query letters. So we included a whole section of Q&A in this book. Whether you're wondering whether you can send unpublished stories as clips or you want to know how to figure out an editor's e-mail address, you can find the answers here. Of course, being a renegade, you know that your mileage may vary. Don't take our word for it ... experiment and do what works best for you!

Armed with this book, you can get into Harvard, have a whiter, brighter smile, and fend off hordes of angry ninjas. Okay, we're exaggerating. But you can break into the magazine of your dreams or boost your writing business. Now get reading!

Section I: Query Letter Q&A

The art and science of querying inspires more questions and debate from writers — especially beginning writers — than any other aspect of magazine writing. Here are our answers to the questions that we typically get. If you don't like our answers, do what we did: dust off your Magic 8 ball in the closet and answer them yourself. (Just kidding.)

Q&A

QShould I mail my query or e-mail it?

A Given a choice between mailing a hard copy of our query letters or e-mailing them, it's really no choice for us: it's e-mail all the way, baby. E-mail has made life so much easier for professional freelancers: you don't have to worry about how your stationery looks or if your ink cartridge is down to its last drop. SASEs (self-addressed stamped envelopes) are relics of the past. Plus, there's the psychological boost you get when you hit the *send* button. Within a millisecond, your damn good query is right where you want it to be — in your editor's inbox (that is, if you've gotten his e-mail address correct). We've gotten responses to our e-mailed queries sometimes in less than five minutes — you can't beat that kind of turnaround. Even if it's to say, "No thanks," the rejection comes fast and we can then get the idea to another editor, pronto. When you drop your letter off at the post office, who knows where that package of paper will end up? Worse, we've found the response rate to snail-mailed queries is far worse than e-mailed queries. Another thing to keep in mind: editors are getting younger. That means e-mail isn't some technological gizmo they need to master — some of these editors have had their own e-mail address since preschool. (Or at least they look young enough.)

Of course, there's no guarantee that if you e-mail your query you'll get a fast response — or any response, for that matter. But when you stack up all the time-saving efficiencies of e-mail against snail mail, e-mail's a no-brainer for the freelancer who wants to make more sales more quickly.

Q What should I put in the subject line of my e-mailed query?

A We use the KISS (keep it simple, sucker!) rule when composing subject lines on e-mailed queries. What works for us is the format of "QUERY: Article subject/Our name." We know writers who amend that format to "WRITER'S QUERY" so that the editor knows the story isn't coming from a PR agency. For the article subject you may want to use key words rather than the actual title ("Safe Dental Fillings for Children") and then your name. The rationale for this system is if the editor has to search her inbox for the idea on dental fillings, she has a better chance with keywords versus a title. Or if she has worked with us before, she can just do a search on our name and *voila*!

(And make sure the subject line makes sense. Once Linda sent out a pitch called "What's That Smell?" using this format, so the subject line was "What's That Smell? Linda Formichelli." Only later did she realize that the way she worded it, her editor probably thought she was confessing to B.O.)

When sending an intro letter to an editor, some writers have success putting something simple like "Business Writer" in the subject line. Linda usually lists two or three of the most pertinent mags she's written for, such as "Writer for Fitness, Women's Health, and Natural Health" for a health magazine or "Writer for Business Advisor, Business Start-Ups, and Target Marketing" for a business pub.

Obviously, you don't want your header to look like spam, which is why it's a good idea to avoid words like "free," "sex," "teens," or "Viagra."

Q&A

Do I need professionally printed stationery?

Gather 'round, and let Linda tell you the story of her history with professionally printed stationery.

Years ago, when I was but a fledgling writer, I sent a query about an interesting woman to a dream market. To look as professional as possible, I printed up the query on the fancy, professionally printed letterhead I used for the copywriting side of my business. A couple of weeks later, I got an e-mail from the editor of my target magazine. She said that she loved the idea — but that she couldn't assign it to me because she suspected, due to my letterhead, that I had been hired by the source to garner her some publicity. Getting paid by both the magazine and the source of your article is a big journalistic no-no. So I lost out on my chance to be published in my dream magazine.

A couple of years later, I shelled out big bucks for three-color stationery and business cards for my magazine writing. I even had a super-duper slogan: "Compelling Content." This was to separate me from the rest of the freelancers out there, who supplied less-than-compelling content.

But by then, I was using e-mail to send 99 percent of my queries. The pricey stationery languished in its box until we moved — and then I chucked it all in the recycling bin.

I may be slow, but I do eventually wise up. Editors don't care about three-color stationery and slogans and logos. All they want are your great ideas and your

I use blank, white résumé paper that I buy in bulk from the office supply store.

mad writing skills. Besides, since you're doing most of your correspondence via e-mail (you are, right?), most editors will never even see that fancy, expensive letterhead.

Now if I'm snail mailing a letter to an editor, I use blank, white

Query Letters that Rock

résumé paper that I buy in bulk from the office supply store. My business cards are black-and-white specials from iPrint (though I do order raised ink — some habits die hard). My editors have not turned up their noses at my plain, cheap-o stationery. That's not to say that professional stationery is bad; I know lots of writers who use it and love it. But don't feel that you have to have it.

If I hadn't bought all that professionally printed letterhead, I would have invested that $500 in some hot stock. Once the stock went through the roof, I would have dumped it, raked in the moolah, and bought a nice cottage in the south of France. Learn from my story, o readers — and in a few years you'll be writing me to say, *merci.*

Q&A

Q What if the guidelines say to snail mail my query?

A What if someone told you to jump off a bridge? Would you do it?

Okay, so snail mailing your query isn't exactly the same as taking a header off the Golden Gate. But they're both actions that require serious consideration.

When you snail mail a query, it often gets opened by an editorial assistant, who tosses it into what's euphemistically termed the "slush pile" along with dozens and dozens of other queries. There it languishes until someone has the time to slog through the pile, sorting the good from the bad. In the meantime, your beautiful query may be lost, mangled, spindled, or mutilated. Your SASE (if you sent one) may get separated from your query.

On the other hand, say you zap your query directly to the assigning editor. It lands right in her hands, no middle man required. Of course, there's no guarantee that the editor will be able to look at it right away, but often you'll hear back in a matter of days or weeks, instead of months (or never) as with snail mail.

But what about the guidelines? Well, we've never had an editor chastise us for sending an e-mail query when the guidelines specify snail mail. In fact, we've heard some editors say that they don't even know what the guidelines are! They're on the lookout for great ideas and super writing, and if something that fits that description lands in their inbox, they won't complain.

What if the guidelines say to e-mail my query to a general editorial mailbox?

In general, sending to a general editorial mailbox is the equivalent of snail mailing your query directly to the slush pile, or addressing your query "Dear Editor." You want to get your idea into the hands of the person who has the power to assign you an article. Do a little research to find the direct e-mail address of the correct editor. If this means calling the editorial offices, do it.

The exception is with tiny magazines that have only one or two editors on staff. Chances are, an actual editor will be checking that general editorial mailbox. And there are a few magazines, such as *Smithsonian* and *mental_floss*, that have online submission forms for writers (and the editors really do answer!).

Q&A

Q **What if the writers' guidelines say "send clips," but I don't have any?**

A When Diana teaches her local freelance writing class, this is the one question that inspires the most anxiety with students. It is a perplexing situation for the beginning freelancer — but it's also a problem even the most successful writers had to overcome early in their careers, so don't go pounding your head against a keyboard yet. No, save the head-banging for the first time you get a third round of revisions on a 200-word short.

The first thing you want to do is focus on writing the best damn query letter you can. Unlike the more established freelancer who can squeak by with great clips supporting a solid idea, your query letter has to have that special something that makes editors forget that pesky little requirement they've stuck in their writers' guidelines to discourage the throngs of wannabes and no-talents from knocking on their doors. At this point in your career, all you've got going for you — at least in an editor's eyes — is your faboo idea and kick-ass writing skills.

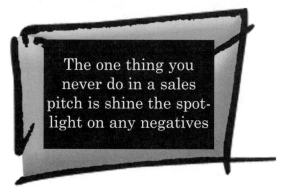

The one thing you never do in a sales pitch is shine the spotlight on any negatives

Of course, you would never do anything so idiotic as to mention in your letter, "I'm sorry, but I'm a new freelancer and don't have any clips to my name. But if you give me an assignment yada, yada, yada." Right? *Right*? A query letter is a sales pitch at heart, and the one thing you never do in a sales pitch is shine the spotlight on any negatives. Can you imagine getting an introductory letter from a local attorney who ends her letter with, "Although I've never had a client, I'm sure I can help you with your next real estate transaction"? Yeah right — you'd be tossing that letter in the recycling bin faster than Paris Hilton ditches fiancés.

Here's what can happen if the editor likes your pitch. She may assume you have clips, and simply give you the assignment. Oh happy day! It has been known to happen and all your bellyaching will be for naught. Diana got her first magazine assignment without the editor asking for clips; however, she did know the assigning editor *and* she had somewhat exclusive access to her subjects.

What's more likely is that the editor will call or e-mail and ask you to send her your clips. Gulp. This is when you'll have to 'fess up. But again, focus on the positive to overcome her objections: "I'm in the process of building my freelance writing career, and don't yet have clips to show you. My ten years as a CPA successfully defending over 1,000 clients before the IRS, however, gives me a unique perspective and background few writers have ...." (Which is why it pays to focus your initial queries on subjects where you have little competition from other writers, because of job experience or exclusive access.)

Occasionally, an editor will balk at giving an assignment to a clipless writer. Some magazines even send clips around among editors for "approval." This happens to the best of us, we're afraid, but the good news is that it tends to happen only with the big national magazines, where they can be picky about writers. To eliminate the risk of this happening, set your sights on smaller markets to build clips while you also aim for the biggies. Or if you're determined to play in the big leagues, pitch shorter stories, which editors may be more willing to assign to a new writer. And remember — Susan Orlean once had no clips.

Q&A

Q **Can I use assigned yet unpublished stories as clips?**

A We know a few writers who've done this and no one has gotten hurt. But we don't do it and we don't think you should, either. Let's say you turned in an assigned story to *SELF* in March, which your editor has said will run at the end of the year. You then pitch *Fitness*, and the editor there asks to see clips. Do you see the problem? Your editor at *SELF* won't be feeling the love for you if she finds out you've provided a competing magazine with copy her magazine plans to run later in the year. Even if the magazines don't compete, it's still not a good practice. The editor who receives your pre-publication clips may ask himself, "Do I want to work with a writer who's this indiscreet with her client's business?" And since editors change jobs faster than they can send out rejection letters, who's to say where this editor will be next month?

There are a couple ways to handle this frustrating situation. You could ask your editor at magazine #1 for permission to show your article to the editor at magazine #2. There's a slight chance she may give you the okay ... perhaps if the other publication is noncompeting or if the article has been sitting around in inventory for ages. Another tack: if the experience with editor #1 went very well, you could ask if she'd vouch for your writing ability and dependability with editors at other magazines ... sort of like asking for a reference. At any rate, be honest with editor #2. In your query letter, you can write, "I've written for *SELF*." When she asks for clips, you could say something like, "My article for *SELF* is running in December, so I'm afraid I don't have the clip to send you. As soon as it runs, I'll be happy to send it. In the meantime, I've received another assignment from *SELF*, as well as *Woman's Day*." (Subtext: I'm hot. Hire me.) An editor's fears of dealing with a new writer may be assuaged knowing you're out there selling; however, if another editor is willing to vouch for your abilities and professionalism, it may be the ticket you need to overcome this dilemma.

Query Letters that Rock

Q **Should I send a self-addressed stamped envelope?**

A This question indicates that you're snail mailing your query. In which case, you should keep in mind our slogan, which was inspired by junior high kids:

"E-mail rules, snail mail drools."

Remember, you should e-mail your query whenever possible. Then, instead of fiddling with your SASE, the editor can simply hit "reply." Also, you save stamps — and trees.

But if, for some crazy reason, you still insist on sending your query via snail mail, you'll need to decide whether to send a SASE or leave it out.

Here we have two opposing camps. One camp says the SASE makes it easier for the editor to respond to your query. The other camp says the SASE is the mark of an amateur. If the editor wants to assign you an article, she'll call or e-mail — and why waste stamps just to collect rejection slips?

That part is true — in ten years of freelance writing, Linda has received just one acceptance via SASE (and that was in 1997). In all other instances, the editors have called or e-mailed to assign the article. So SASEs are basically a means of transporting rejection from the magazine to your house. Who needs that?

On the other hand, if you don't send a SASE, you have no way of knowing if the editor didn't reply because she rejected your idea — or because your query got lost in the mail or slid down behind the staff refrigerator. If you track your queries and like to know when they've been rejected, a SASE is the way to go. If you don't care, leave it out.

Q&A

How much should I research before sending a query letter?

We know successful writers who do very little research on their stories prior to sending a query. Their argument is that they don't want to waste a lot of time researching a story that may never sell. When they get the assignment — and smell the scent of money wafting through the air — they do their research.

We've all heard stories about writers — mainly famous writers — who've told their editors, "I want to write about rocks." Period. And walked away with a $10,000 assignment and an expense account up the yin-yang. In other instances, the editor and writer have a long history and good working relationship, so the editor can place faith in the writer's ability to get a story. However, in most cases, especially for beginning freelancers, editors want to see solid research and reporting in queries. For one thing, it shows that the writer has basic reporting skills. It also shows them there's actually a story to report.

Great, you're muttering to yourself. The editor gets all the benefit. *Au contraire*. We find that doing some good, solid research on our stories well before the guarantee of an assignment gets us an assignment. How's that again? When we spend the time to write up a tight, well-thought-out query letter — getting our facts and figures in place, suggesting an angle for our initial reporting — it virtually guarantees us an assignment. Maybe not the first, second or third time we send it out, but usually these queries sell faster than the pitches that include little reporting.

Take heed of one writer's philosophy about pre-query research if you frequently develop ADD — Assignment Disappointment Disorder. New York City-based freelancer Alison Stein Wellner works by the adage, "You have to give yourself the assignment before you get the assignment." Another benefit of researching a story before querying: "I can find out if I'm interested enough," she says. "If I get bored sniffing around before an assignment, then there's no way I'm interested enough to write the story on assignment. My interest is not going to increase; my curiosity is not for sale."

So the question: How much reporting? You have to do enough research to answer your editor's initial questions: Why is this story important or relevant to our readership? Is there any proof behind the thesis of the article? Is there enough there *there* to pay a writer $1.50/word to commission the story? What questions will the article answer with further research?

Sometimes writers can go a little crazy with initial reporting; if that's you, you have to figure out a way to stop when you have enough to pull together a thoughtful proposal versus a doctoral thesis. Diana, a compulsive researcher, knows your pain. She frequently does huge amounts of research prior to assignment; she's ruthless, however, about homing in on the points that strengthen the sales element of her proposals.

At the very least, do enough research to show why your story is relevant to the magazine. If you can do that with a half-hour of library or Internet research, great. On the other hand, it may take you six phone calls, two interviews, and a field trip. If that's what it takes to get your query letter to where it needs to be, suck it up and do the work. Our experience shows you'll recover your time investment down the road.

Q&A

Q Do I need to pre-interview sources for my query?

A If you plan to have quotes in your article, it's a great idea to have them in your query, too. Many editors want to see that you can find good sources and that you know how to conduct an interview and get compelling quotes. Besides, quotes add a little *je ne sais quois* (that's French for "something that makes the editor want to hire you and pay you a boatload of money to boot") to your query.

It's a conundrum (that's Latin for "annoying writing problem"): How do you get expert sources to agree to talk to you when you don't have an assignment in hand?

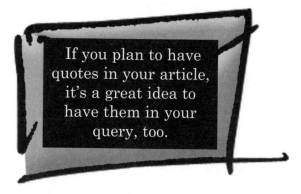

If you plan to have quotes in your article, it's a great idea to have them in your query, too.

When e-mailing or calling a potential source, describe your idea and ask the source to participate in a very quick e-mail or phone interview "just to get a few good quotes for the proposal." Add that you'll be back in touch should you sell the idea. That way the source doesn't waste a lot of time answering your questions when there's no guarantee of publicity.

Also, play up your credentials. If you've been published in other magazines, let the source know. If you have a special expertise in the topic, shout it out. By doing this, you'll build the source's confidence in your ability to actually sell your idea to a magazine, and boost the likelihood that he'll say yes to an interview.

Q How can I find expert sources to quote in my query letter?

A You could try leaning out your window and hollering, but that's unlikely to work unless you live above a nutritionist/doctor/personal trainer/economist/psychiatrist who's willing to shout back an anecdote or two. No, a better way to suss out those sources in your time of need is to use the resources listed below:

Associations

You probably remember this saying from childhood: "Two's company, three's an association of experts willing to speak to the media."

No matter what subject you're researching, from competitive eating (International Federation of Competitive Eating: ifoce.com) to tug of war (Tug of War International Foundation: tugofwar-twif.org), there's undoubtedly an association ready to supply you with experts. After all, the association exists to promote its industry and its members, so it should have a list of media-friendly experts and participants who can tell you everything you need to know about whatever it is you're writing about.

Linda writes often about health, nutrition and fitness, for example, and over the years she's spoken with numerous experts from the American Dietetic Association and the American Council on Exercise. When she wrote about more specialized topics such as sleep snafus and the merits of sea salt, she found the info she needed through the National Sleep Foundation and the Salt Institute.

Finding these groups often takes no more than a Google search on "association," "foundation," or "organization" plus the topic you're working on, such as "automobile." Another place to search is the directory on the American Society of Association Executives Web site: www.asaenet.org. Once you find an association that looks promising, call and ask for the media relations, publicity, or public relations department. Small associations for niche topics might not have a separate department for media relations, but the receptionist can likely guide you to the person within the organization most likely to help you.

Expert Source Sites

Thanks to sites like Yearbook.com and Profnet (profnet.com), you can bypass the associations and go straight to the experts. Yearbook.com is incredibly easy to use and lets you search for sources by subject matter. ProfNet also lets you search for experts, but you must first register with the site; that extra bit of trouble is worth it, though, as ProfNet also lets you send a request for sources (labeled a "query" by ProfNet) to its membership of businesses, think tanks, hospitals, government agencies, and PR firms, either within the U.S. or throughout the world. (Note: You must show you're a published journalist to register.)

Newspapers and Magazines

If you're an aspiring freelance writer, you probably read tons of magazines and newspapers to stay on top of the news and generate ideas. In addition to providing you with reading material, these publications can also provide you with sources for your own articles. Linda had just scored an assignment for an article on perfectionism, for instance, when she ran across an article on the same topic in another publication. One of the sources in that article had recently published a book on the topic, so Linda hunted her down and scored an interview.

Two warnings about this practice: 1) Don't interview an expert who just appeared in a directly competing publication; if an article in, say, *Fitness* used this expert, *SELF* or *Shape* probably won't want to appear like laggards who copy everything *Fitness* does. 2) Research the source to make sure that he or she hasn't been appearing in every single magazine on the newsstands. Editors tire of seeing the same names again and again.

Amazon.com

How do you know someone's an expert? He wrote the book on the topic. And where can you go to find all things bookish? Amazon.com, which catalogues thousands of books on thousands of subjects. When Linda had an assignment about resilience, she searched Amazon.com for all sorts of titles on the topic, including variations on the word such as "resilient" and "resiliency." Bingo! Two book authors became key sources for her article.

Once you locate a book author who seems right for your piece, plug her name into Google and start searching. The author might have a personal Web site including a phone number or e-mail address. If the search comes up blank, try entering www.authors-name.com into your browser, as the author might have registered her own name as a Web domain.

Although contacting the author directly is the best course of action, sometimes the search will draw a blank. When this happens, call the publisher, ask for the media department, and pass along your request for an interview with author X. Publishers crave this kind of attention, so you're sure to hear back from the author — and you'll probably even receive a free copy of the book in the meantime.

Universities

Colleges are designed to churn out experts on all sorts of topics — and they do this by employing folks who already are experts, experts who will often be willing to speak with the press to show their bosses how valuable they really are. So if you need a lawyer, turn to Harvard Law School; a doctor, Harvard Medical School; a waste expert; Harvard Sewage School. Non-Harvard universities will also welcome your call, so don't feel you have to stick with the stuffed shirts in Cambridge.

To find universities that can help you with your assignment, visit the Newswise Contact Directory at www.newswise.com-/resources/ncd/ and use the pull-down menu to select a subject ranging from agriculture to technology.

Q&A

How do I find good anecdotes or quotes from real people to use in my query letter?

You've found a new study that shows women who make love with their husbands more than three times a week live longer and suffer lower rates of depression than women who avoid the horizontal bop. You're excited because it gives you a good story idea for a target market, but you know this magazine likes to begin articles with compelling anecdotes. Where on earth are you going to find a woman who scores low on her lackluster sex life — all for the pleasure of helping you score an assignment?

The answer is easy: ask everyone you know — your friends, your mother, your sister-in-law, the woman who undresses next to you at the gym. Tell them you're developing a proposal and you wondered if they had a story they'd be willing to share. You'll be surprised by the results. Sometimes they don't have a good story, but they know someone who does. You don't have to tell them exactly what your query is about — say, "I'm looking for a married woman who's willing to talk about her sex life for a story proposal I'm working up."

We know several smart, successful freelancers — and we put ourselves in this category — who have an address book of possible sources set up in their e-mail programs. Periodically they e-mail their sources with a list of stories they're researching or working on and ask that these people forward their request on to anyone who may be able to help.

Another strategy — and admittedly it's kind of calculating — is to tell all your friends who fit the magazine's demographics about the study. Maybe one of them will say, "Hmm, that's interesting. I went off Prozac last year when my husband and I started having more sex." You could casually ask, "Hey, I'm thinking about pitching a story to a magazine on this topic and I would love to use your anecdote. Mind if I use it in my letter?" We know other writers who don't ask — they take the anecdote and run. Once they have an assignment in hand, they ask their potential source if they can use the story. If they get a no, they look for another anecdote from someone else. Beware: if you have a terrible memory like Diana, this strategy can backfire. You could be putting a friendship at risk if you forget to check the anecdote with your source and it makes its way to the magazine's factchecker — or worse, print.

As for your editors, half the time they don't notice if your anecdote happens to be different in the finished piece. If this does become an issue, you can tell them the original source backed out.

If you're still having trouble finding quotes and anecdotes for your queries, there are always places like ProfNet. We've had good luck landing the wily source by casting our request into a pool of PR professionals, many of whom love speaking to the press even on a personal topic. Again, keep your quest vague enough so that your idea can't be poached (there are plenty of authors and journalists who are ProfNet subscribers) and explain you're looking for anecdotes for a story you're researching, not an assignment in hand.

Q&A

Q **I'm pitching a story about bedwetters, and my anecdote comes from my sister. Should I mention the relationship in my query letter?**

A If you're using the anecdote in your query letter, but don't intend to include it in your article, then there's no need to mention the connection. When you get the assignment, you can ask your editor how she feels about using relatives. Some publications don't mind — but others have rules about that stuff, so do ask. If it's in the magazine's style to talk about relatives, you could say, "My sister told me last week that my nephew ...."

The other thing to consider is how your sister will feel if her anecdote makes it to print. It's one thing to tell you, her brother or sister, about her son's bedwetting, but another to share it with the world. Sometimes potential sources don't realize what it's like to see their name and story in print until it's on the newsstand — and even though they gave you permission to share the story, they later regret it, causing some bad blood. Some writers we know have a policy of not using friends and relatives in their stories; this may be a good policy for you if you've run into prickly situations with your friends and family in the past.

Q What's the difference between a "pitch," a "query," and a "proposal"?

A An editor phones to say she loves your pitch on nude beaches on the Alaskan coast ... now she wants a full proposal. Another editor says he liked your proposal on career opportunities in gravedigging, although said proposal was offered during a phone call. Some writers — and editors — use the words interchangeably. Others see slight differences.

"My take is that they're a little bit different, but they all get at the same thing: I'm selling something and I want you to buy it," says Ted Spiker, assistant professor at the University of Florida's College of Journalism and Communications. "The pitch is the informal, I-already-know-the-editor, general idea for a story, 'Hey, Bob, I'm thinking about doing something on gravediggers. I'm snooping around to find a few angles, but here are a few things I had in mind....' I see it as a little less developed,

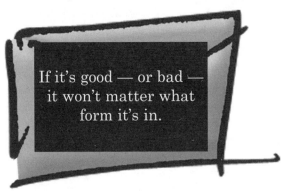

If it's good — or bad — it won't matter what form it's in.

maybe a not-quite-formed idea that the writer is dangling in front of the editor to see if there might be enough interest to develop something more specific. The query is the formal, traditional, one-idea letter with catchy lede as an opener, development of what the story would be, and then the close. A proposal is closer to a full outline. What's the hook? The angle? The sources? How is it chunked up, if it's a chunky story? What specifically are the 10 entry points (in a '10 ways to do x' story)? In a way, it's almost developed enough so it could serve as an art memo once it's initially approved as a story."

Sarah Smith, articles editor at *Parenting*, says, "They're so similar that we wouldn't think anyone was using the wrong term in any particular context, but there's a subtle difference in my reaction to the words." For example, she considers the initial correspondence from a new-to-her writer as a "query," because the document is not only selling an idea, but also the writer. "I don't tend to think of writers I know well sending me queries," she explains. "They send me pitches and proposals." An interesting pitch — a couple lines about a story idea — from an established writer will probably result in Smith replying, "Sounds good, send me a proposal," the fleshed-out story idea that circulates among other *Parenting* editors for approval. However she adds, "If a writer I've worked with before asks, 'Can I send you a query?' it wouldn't occur to me to say, 'No, what I need is a proposal.'"

So pitch, proposal, query ... which is it? If you're confused by your editor's request for a "proposal" when you sent her what you thought was a query jam-packed with juicy details, ask her what additional information she'd like from you. Perhaps she wants to know precisely how many nude beaches there are in Alaska or the names of some of the more popular hot spots. If another editor likes your "pitch," but you sent in a query, there's no need to work yourself up into a tizzy over word choice. Spiker, who's also a contributing editor for *Men's Health* and an editor-at-large for *Women's Health*, says, "Writers don't really need to worry about the semantics. They just need to worry about getting the good idea, because if it's good — or bad — it won't matter what form it's in."

How long should my query letter be?

As long as it needs to be to show the editor that you have a great idea, you know how to research, you're an outstanding writer, and you have what it takes to write the article. This may take one paragraph; it may take three pages.

Three pages!? All the other books command that queries be no longer than one page. What gives?

Here's where we tell the well-worn story of how Linda broke into the women's magazine market. In the late nineties she churned out one-page queries just as all the writing books demanded, but had no success breaking into the coveted women's magazines. Then, one day, an editor took pity on Linda and told her that she would have a better chance of acceptance if her queries contained more research. So Linda researched her little heart out, and included expert quotes, statistics, and examples in her queries. All this information caused her queries to bloat to an unheard-of three pages.

Surprise! Those three-pagers landed Linda assignments with *Family Circle*, *Woman's Day*, and *Redbook*, all within a couple of months.

That's not to say all queries must rival Yongle Dadian (the longest book in the history of the world — look it up!). Especially if you've already worked with an editor, you can sometimes get away with the bare minimum. Heck, Linda has sold articles based on two-sentence queries!

The point is, don't let the one-page-query mandate get you down. With experience, you'll learn just how much information you need to include in your queries to score an assignment.

Q&A

Q **Is it okay to dash off a quick note to an editor about a potential story idea before I invest the time in a full-blown proposal?**

A We do this all the time with our editors. With two editors at one magazine, Diana has written up bulleted lists of story ideas with one or two lines explaining the angle. Her editors get back to her with quick "yeas," "nays," or suggestions on different angles. Even better are the times when she can schedule a phone call with her editors to talk ideas. The immediate feedback means she doesn't waste time on ideas that won't fly, and she can get to work — fast — on the promising ones.

Linda does the same. She frequently sends quick ideas to her editors — such as, "I just read about a new study that shows that babies can be altruistic. Would you be interested in a story on this research?" — and the editors say either "yes," "no," or "send a proposal."

This strategy usually works only when you have worked with an editor before. If you've done a couple stories for a magazine, ask if it's okay to do this. Honestly, most editors are kind people, and when they know you're a dedicated professional, they don't want you to waste your time, either.

If you are approaching an editor for the first time, chances are this strategy won't work. A query letter for many editors is less about selling an idea and more a calling card for a writer. They'll want to see the full-blown proposal and simply don't have time to prescreen ideas for new-to-them freelancers.

Q How do I pick the right editor to send my query letter to? How do I find out who edits the section I want to write for?

A There are a couple of ways to crack this nut. The easiest, yet least accurate, way is to look at the magazine. If you're pitching a feature article, is there an articles editor or features editor on the masthead? If you're pitching a department story, sometimes the department sections include the editor's name ("Edited by Jane Smith"). The reason this is the least accurate way is that mastheads are often out of date by the time they hit the stands.

A more accurate way to get what you need is dialing the magazine's main switchboard and asking for the editorial department. You'll probably get routed to an editorial assistant. Simply ask:

"I'm getting ready to send a health-related query for a feature. Who's the right editor for this kind of story?"

or

"I'm checking to make sure John Jones is still editing the Departures department. Is that correct?"

or

"I have an idea for a short I'd like to send to the editor who handles the Departures section. Would you tell me who assigns for this department?"

Editorial assistants get these calls all the time — it's part of their job to handle inquiries from writers — so don't work yourself up into a sweat. Keep your call short and sweet and you'll be fine. Ninety-five percent of the time you'll get the information you need in a minute or less. The other five percent of the time, you'll either go into voicemail hell or, rarely, get someone on the line who's either clueless or off his meds that day. Even more rarely will you get someone who'll demand to know what your story is about. Not to hurt your feelings, but the person picking up the phone that day probably doesn't give a fig about your story idea and won't bother to ask — which means you shouldn't bother sharing it, either.

If these strategies don't work, post your question on a writers' bulletin board like Mediabistro (www.mediabistro.com) or Freelance Success (www.freelancesuccess.com). A "Who edits the Baby Time section at magazine X" should get you a name, which you can then check with a quick phone call after hours by using the dial-by-name directory.

Q Should I err on the side of formality with my salutation ("Dear Ms. Smith") or be informal ("Dear Joe")?

A Really, it's a personal preference. If it feels strange to you to call someone by his first name, then go with Mister. There are certainly a few editors who appreciate the etiquette of a formal title. On the other hand, editors are getting younger and younger. Calling a 24-year-old editorial assistant Mr. Jones may remind him of his dad. Or his grandfather down in Boca Raton.

Our solution is to look to the magazine for guidance. What's the magazine's tone? Who's their audience? We'd go for informal when pitching a magazine like *Details* or *SELF* but skip the "Hey Dave!" when pitching *The New Yorker*.

When you start a communication with an editor, follow her lead. If you send your pitch to "Dear Ms. Smith" and in her reply she calls you by your first name, you can do the same in subsequent messages (using her first name, not yours, silly).

Q&A

Q **What's the best day to send a query?**

A Diana wondered this early in her career, but years of sending queries out seven days a week have shown her there's no one better day than another to hit the send button. She once sent a query on a Saturday afternoon and received a favorable response from a women's magazine editor on a Sunday night. She has sent queries to editors who were supposedly having slow weeks and heard nothing until she nudged them from their stupor several weeks later.

Our advice is to hit the send button once your query is ready to go. A great idea, well written, will always rise to the top with the right editor, no matter what day of the week it lands in his inbox.

Q How do I find an editor's e-mail address if it's not published?

A This is where we get sneaky! Check out the various ways you can sleuth out an editor's unpublished e-mail address:

Call and ask. Okay, this one is not so sneaky, but it should be your first tactic. You can often find a magazine's phone number in Writer's Market, in the magazine's masthead, or on the magazine's Web site. If those sources turn up empty, look up the magazine publisher's main number in an online business directory such as hoovers.com. For, example, if you're looking to call *Cosmopolitan*, dig up the main number for Hearst. Tell the receptionist that you're looking for the editorial department for *Cosmopolitan*, and she'll connect you or give you the phone number.

Check the advertising department. Surf to the mag's Web site and click onto the page for advertisers. The ad rep will often have an e-mail address listed, and from that you can figure out the magazine's e-mail format. For example, if the magazine's ad rep is listed as jane_doe@magazine.com, you can surmise that you can reach the editors using the format firstname_lastname@magazine.com.

Check the databases. If you belong to sites like Freelance Success (www.freelancesuccess.com), you can access their databases of magazines' e-mail formats.

Ask around. If you know someone who writes for the magazine you're targeting, ask him to do you a solid and pass along the editor's e-mail address. If you're not so lucky, ask on your fave online writing forum for the e-mail format. Be sure to explain the lengths you've already gone to to find the address, so readers don't think you're shirking your research.

Guess. As a last resort, you can take your best shot at guessing the magazine's e-mail format. If the editor's name is Ima Neditor, first try sending your query to ieditor@magazine.com. If that bounces back, try imaneditor@magazine.com. No luck? Move on to ima.neditor@magazine.com, then ima_neditor@magazine.com and so on. This may not seem like the best approach, but years ago Linda got in contact with an editor at *National Geographic* using this tactic!

Q How can I find out if an editor is a guy or girl?

A Especially if you're erring toward formality in your salutation to Chris Smith ("Dear Mr. Smith"), how can you be 100 percent sure you've got XY chromosomes at the other end of your correspondence? Names like Chris and Alex just scratch the surface. Dana? Leslie? Diana has a sister-in-law named Shawn and uncles named Robin and Kim. She has a brother-in-law named Randy and a female friend named ... Randy. You get the picture — it can be easy to make gender assumptions about names.

We're assuming you won't get the opportunity to sneak a peek down your editor's boxers or panties, so here are some other ways to perform non-scientific sex determination tests. You can always call the editor after hours and see what the voice sounds like on his or her voicemail — although voice isn't always a guarantee (and the editor may have had his or her assistant record the outgoing message). You can also call the magazine's switchboard and ask, or inquire amongst your writer buddies. The safest bet? Keep your salutation gender-neutral with "Dear Chris Smith."

Q&A

Q Can I send the same query out to different publications?

A Of course — you can do anything you want!† You can eat peanut butter and bacon sandwiches, you can wear plaid with stripes, and you can send the same query out to different magazines. Besides residing in the Land of the Free, you need to make a living — and it's hard to do that if you have to wait months for each magazine to get back to you before you can send your query along to the next.

The real question is, should you? You want to strike a delicate balance between getting your query into as many editorial hands as possible as quickly as possible and avoiding having editors of two competing magazines accept your idea at the same time. So ask yourself these questions:

Do you have an "in" at any of your target magazines? If you've written for an editor before, or even if she has only encouraged you to send in more ideas in her rejection notes, you have an in. Since she's more inclined than an editor who doesn't know you from Adam to look at your query and give you a speedy response, you may want to give this editor an exclusive look at your idea.

Are there any "fast responders" on your list? If your list of target editors includes any that have proven to be fast responders — for example, if *Dream Magazine* always responds to your queries within two days — it won't hurt to send your query to one at a time and wait the short time for a response.

Are you an experienced freelancer? Freelancers who are known in the industry often command faster query response times — and more acceptances — than newer writers. For example, if you've written for *Fortune, Forbes, Business 2.0,* and *Fast Company,* and you're

---

† We're assuming here that you understand that you'll always need to tweak your query for each magazine; don't spam identical queries to every editor on the planet.

targeting business magazines, chances are greater that (1) you'll get a quick response, and (2) you'll land an assignment. It's safer to send your query to one editor at a time.

Now, if you're pitching a bunch of magazines cold — that is, you don't know them and they don't know you — knock yourself out! For example, if you're trying to break into the women's magazine market and the editors know you about as well as you know the square root of 674123.9, then go ahead and send your query out to all of your markets at once.

Q&A

Why can't I skip the query and just write the article for the magazine?

When an editor wants you to write an article, he'll tell you the slant he wants you to take, the word count, and sometimes even the sources he'd like you to interview. Often, these requirements are different from what you'd pitched in your query. For example, say you pitch a 2,000-word profile of a woman who started a business painting wall murals in kids' rooms. The editor calls you and says, "I like this idea, but I can give you only 1,200 words. Also, I'd like you to find and interview two other women who have made businesses out of products and services for kids." It happens all the time.

Knowing this, what are the chances that an article you write without the editor's input will be just the right slant, and be just the right word length, and have just the right sources? You may think that writing a query is a waste of time, but writing an entire article without an assignment is an even bigger waste of time. You can't read an editor's mind, so don't even try.

As with all things, there are always exceptions. Editors generally like to see the entire manuscript for personal essays, because it's difficult to get an idea of the writer's story and style from a query letter. Also, a few magazines do ask writers to send articles "on spec," meaning they want to see the article and then they'll decide whether to send you a contract (and money). If a magazine prefers to see articles on spec, this information will usually be in the magazine's writer's guidelines or in Writer's Market. (And whether you should write on spec at all is a controversial topic among writers.)

If you're querying a very short piece — say, 300 words or under — and you're so excited about the idea that you just can't help but write it, go ahead. This is how Linda broke into *Details* and *Psychology Today*. But a safer bet is to write out a short query and shoot it over to the editor via e-mail.

Q Forget writing query letters — can I get an assignment by sending a letter of introduction, clips, and a résumé to an editor?

A Maybe this tactic works if you're a world-famous magazine writer, but if you're a regular schlumpf like the rest of us, sending introductory packets to magazine editors will probably net you a lot of copying and postage costs for little return — with a few notable exceptions.

Consumer magazines already have stables of strong writers in place. It's really, really hard to convince an editor through an introduction letter and résumé that you should become her new go-to guy or gal. The best way to convince her of this is by building a relationship — one query letter at a time.

When asked about receiving an introduction package from a new-to-her writer, Kristin Godsey, editor of *Writer's Digest*, said this: "Personally, I don't like this at all. It strikes me as kind of lazy, as in, 'Here I am! I have nothing specific to offer you, but call me with an assignment anytime!' The exceptions are if (a) you've got some absolutely outstanding credentials in terms of freelance clips, like *The New York Times* or several major national magazines and you're willing to work for our pay rate; (b) you've got celebrity status in my magazine's field (in other words, Stephen King, feel free to send me a letter of intro and clips), or (c) you're willing to write for free (and even in this case, you should still have solid credentials and good clips). But otherwise, I'm going to toss your letter unless you've got a strong, thought-out idea tailored to my magazine. I'm very unlikely to assign a feature idea I have (or someone on my

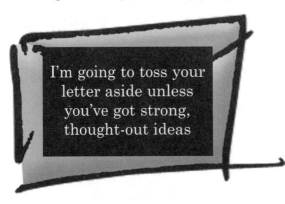

I'm going to toss your letter aside unless you've got strong, thought-out ideas

staff has) to someone I've never worked with. I'll go to someone I know for a fact can do the job." Sarah Smith, articles editor at *Parenting*, has a similar viewpoint. She says, "Just because you're available isn't enough for me. I need to know you understand us and have good ideas."

Trade magazines, custom publications, and regional magazines and newspapers, on the other hand, may welcome an introduction letter, résumé, and clips from a writer. Many of these magazines, especially the trade publications, generate their story ideas in-house and some of them struggle to find writers who understand the magazine's demographic. If you worked for ten years in wastewater management, then editors at magazines covering this industry will probably fall over themselves getting back to you, especially if you're articulate and can demonstrate a basic understanding of their magazine.

Many writers pooh-pooh trades — they're not as glamorous as the magazines on your local newsstand. But if you don't want to query and you do want to eat, adding trade magazines to your mix of clients is a good way to go.

Cara McDonald, deputy editor of *5280*, recalls that a senior editor from a national magazine moved to Denver and contacted her about writing for her magazine: "We got them right in here and gave them a job," she says. That kind of experience at the national level can be irresistible for regional magazines, which often win as many top magazine awards as the big boys (and girls) on Madison Avenue.

But if you're starting out, or you're building your career as, say, a health writer for national women's magazines, pitching strong, well-written ideas will be your best way to assignments. Leave the intro letters for later on in your career.

Q I have some really great credentials for the article I'm pitching; should I list them first or put them at the end of my query?

A Definitely get them in first thing for two reasons: First, it'll get the editor to really take notice of your actual idea. One of the big questions an editor has when she's reading through a query is "Why is this writer the right person to write this story?" If you're pitching an article to a scientific magazine on new space vehicles NASA has developed, it would probably be a good thing to note in the first sentence that you're a former astronaut-turned-science-writer, if indeed this is the case. And second, even if the idea isn't quite right for them — they just did a piece on space vehicles, for example — they may have other articles they would love to assign to a former-astronaut-turned-science-writer.

This very scenario happened to Diana a few months ago when she pitched an editor at a new health magazine. The first thing she mentioned in her query was that she had authored a book on the psychology of weight loss. The editor got right back to her, excited not about the idea she pitched, but the fact she'd written a book about dieting and did she have any story ideas along those lines?

When Linda sends queries, she often opens the e-mail with a quick paragraph stating her creds, hoping to dazzle the editors with her national publications. She then pastes the query below.

Q&A

Can I submit a killed article to a new magazine?

You've probably sweated through two or three revisions, so nothing would feel better than to send the finished piece to another magazine. The bad news is that you still need to write up a query for your next market. The good news is, of course, you probably had to write a query for the magazine that killed your story, so you're halfway — maybe even 7/8ths of the way — there. You'll have to change a name and address, and maybe reslant the query a bit to appeal to a different readership. You may have even learned some things when you were reporting the story that would make a new query even stronger. The even better news is if you land an assignment, your article may be good to go! Which brings us to ....

Should I mention in my query letter that this story was killed by a competing publication?

Let's put it this way: How thrilled would you be to learn that your significant other hooked up with you because your best friend wouldn't touch him or her with a barge pole? You should know that magazine editors find the thought of sloppy seconds so distasteful that only a confirmed masochist would enlighten them that their story has already been worked over and massaged so hard by another magazine that it died a painful death. It's old history only you — and maybe your accountant and psychoanalyst — need to know.

When should I follow up on a query letter?

You proofread your pitch dozens of times before you hit send, and now a whole day has passed. All that's showing up in your in-box is e-mail from Mr. Moses Odiaka in Nigeria, whose sincerest wish is to wire you $18.5 million — if you'll kindly provide him with your checking account's routing number. Time to pick up the phone and call the slacking editor?

Even though developments in electronic communications have made life much nicer for freelancers, the fact is, business still moves at a snail's pace at most magazines. Even if your editor has had a chance to read your pitch, he still needs time to consider it — not to mention that assigning a story is usually not a one-person job. He'll probably forward your query to other editors for approval. Or he simply may need a few days to consider the idea. Or even more likely, he's probably up to his Men's Club hairpiece putting a current issue of the magazine together or suffering through another all-day staff development meeting. Nothing will irritate him more than to return to his office, check his voicemail, and hear some whiny voice complain, "I sent you a query letter on the danger of air fresheners yesterday. Why haven't you responded? Please call me at blah-blah-blah."

We know a few successful writers who follow up on e-mailed pitches in five business days

We know a few successful writers who follow up on e-mailed pitches in five business days when they haven't heard a peep from the editor. Other writers we know give the editor two or three weeks. (And still others never follow up, which is just crazy. Crazy!) So the answer is, What time frame feels comfortable to you? If your ideas are time sensitive, you indeed should follow up in a day or two. In this case, you should stress in your letter that the story is time-sensitive, and if you don't hear back by a certain time, you and your hot story about a closeted Hollywood superstar we'll call I. Cure Most will be moving on to greener pastures. If it's a pitch on an evergreen topic, a week or two is a safer — and saner — bet.

What's fairly common with a good idea is that you'll get a quick response from the editor, who'll tell you he wants to bring the idea to his next story meeting or circulate it among the other editors for approval. Oh joy! Usually, he won't give you any idea how long this process can take — so ask. If he says his story meeting is at the end of the month, tell him when you'll call if you don't hear from him. Many times he simply won't know how long, so let him know you'll plan to follow up in two or three weeks — then follow up! In our experience, an acceptance or rejection can come as quickly as a few days — or (more likely), a few months. Editors generally don't mind a nudge or a quick follow-up … pleasant persistence is a good thing in this business. But calling every day about air freshener safety? Stop it right now.

Q How should I follow up on a query letter — phone or e-mail?

A A lot of writers we know have major phone phobia, especially with editors. Maybe it's because editors spend a lot of time trying to convince writers they're horribly busy, and we hesitate to interrupt their stressful, important jobs of putting a monthly magazine together. It sort of feels like calling a neurosurgeon during brain surgery — the thought terrifies. (And yes, we're being snarky.)

The good news about e-mail followups is that you can paste your initial pitch into the document, giving the editor a reference point. She doesn't have to riffle through her inbasket looking for your earlier correspondence. If you phone, chances are good an editor's not going to remember the details of your pitch, unless she happens to have it right in front of her.

So our advice is to do your initial followups via e-mail. If you don't get a response, you can either assume the editor's not interested or decide to pick up the phone and get more personal. On the other hand, if the editor has gotten back to you — she's interested, but waiting for her next story meeting to present your idea — we advise following up with a phone call. It's a great way to put a voice to a name, and who knows — you may be calling at the exact time she needs a writer to handle a quick assignment.

Like all professionals, editors don't want to be pestered. If you call someone every day, she's going to start thinking of you as a stalker, not a writer. Don't leave threatening messages if you get her voicemail ("I'm going to keep calling you every day at noon until you pick up and give me an answer"). She'll give you an answer, all right — bug off, creep. If she says she doesn't know when she'll have an answer, ask her, "Can I follow up with you on [date] if I don't hear from you before then, or will that be too soon?"

Q&A

QWhat if, despite my followups, an editor doesn't respond to my query? When should I move on?

AThere are some editors who still think rejections are the worst thing freelancers face. No, the cold shoulder is even worse. Certainly no one likes to hear no, but a no is better than a persistent echo in our e-mail inboxes. This is one of the biggest gripes we hear from professional writers. Editors are busy people, for sure, but how long would it take them to type out a quick, "No thanks" or "We're still thinking about this ... check back in two weeks"?

When we're sitting around waiting for editors to make decisions on our stories, it can be frustrating. That's why it's a good idea to plan ahead of time how you'll conduct followups on queries that are MIA. If the idea is timely, you can say something like, "Would you let me know by May 10 if you're interested in this story?"

The problem is — and it's a good problem to have — editors will often show initial interest in the idea and ask to bring it to an editorial meeting or show it around the office. There's usually no clear timeline when this will happen, though, so your idea is out of commission until you hear back.

Freelancers cope in a variety of ways. Some have a three-strikes-and-it's-on-to-the-next-magazine rule, figuring that if they've heard nothing, the editor's not interested. Others don't give up on an editor until they get a firm answer — which sometimes can take dozens of e-mails and phone calls, to the point where it feels like stalking. Unbelievably, we've heard stories where the editor has come to after months and months of followup and commissioned the story, so if you like the chase, go for it. We know other writers who don't follow up at all — and are surprised a year later when the editor calls out of the blue. Still others pitch the idea to multiple editors and let the early bird get the worm. The bottom line is that there's no firm answer for when to move on — you've got to pick a system that works for you, and this will take trial and error.

Q **I requested a return receipt on my e-mailed query. It's been two weeks and I don't think she has opened my e-mail. What should I do?**

A Personally, we hate it when people send us e-mail and a little message pops up asking if it's okay to send a return receipt that we've read their note blasting us for encouraging writers to banish one-page query letters. We're curmudgeons — we always click No, it's not okay. It's nosy is what it is. But we digress.

Why torture yourself with wondering why an editor read your query at 8:58 a.m. on Monday morning, and now it's Tuesday afternoon and you don't even have cold, gelatinous spam sitting in your inbox? But you've gone ahead and done this with an editor and found out she's as curmudgeonly as we are. She seemingly has tossed your query aside without a glance — or worse, deleted it. Rather than come back at her with a virtual tire iron when you do your follow-ups, follow up on your query as you normally would, making no mention of the return receipt (or lack thereof) on your first go-round. It'll just make you sound like a stalkerazzi. If, despite your numerous followups, she never responds to your query, you can assume two things: first, return receipts don't make a lick of difference to her and second, neither does the simple courtesy of a "no thanks." Move on.

Q&A

Q **My editor liked my query letter, but she wants me to "flesh it out." Should I ask for money?**

A Your editor is asking you to "flesh out" your idea because there isn't enough information there for her to make a decision to assign. Says Kristin Godsey, editor of *Writer's Digest*, "If you send me a 'query' that says, 'I'd like to write a piece on the pros and cons of writing articles on spec,' I'm going to want to know what some of those pros and cons are. How do I know you know what you're talking about otherwise? And how else would I know if you're just going to give me the same old, same old clichéd advice everyone always hears?"

We feel it's not the smartest thing for writers to ask for money if your editor has a few questions about your story. She's interested enough to come back to you with some questions, to give you a chance to score a sale ... so just answer her questions as compellingly as you can and assume you'll recover your time when you get the assignment.

The problem is when an editor keeps coming back to you with question after question, as Diana experienced a few years back with a national women's magazine. Though her query letter was detailed, Diana felt a few questions from the editor were understandable. However, after a period of weeks, the questions became answerable only through interviews with the source. It was really time for the magazine to make an assignment at this point. She should have asked her editor at this point to either fish or cut bait.

My editor asked me to develop a story based on her idea. Should I ask for money?

Magazines are businesses. They don't want to spend any more money than they have to, which means they try to pinch pennies like any smart business does. Certainly this is the case when editors have some great ideas and want to find out if the ideas have legs enough to stand. Why not have a freelancer do the research? Dangle the hint of an assignment in front of them, and these suckers will pretty much do anything!

We have it on good authority that a couple of big-name magazines regularly "assign" ideas for freelancers to research. When all the research comes on, the editors pick and choose from the proposals. At one magazine, sometimes up to a dozen freelancers are working on the same story.

And even if you're dealing with one of the majority of editors who are clean and pure, the bad news is that you're still spending time on a project that may not fly. If you've worked with your editor a lot, you may have a track record where you know these kinds of proposals always lead to an assignment: the proposal is just a formality. In other cases, it's not so cut and dry. We feel that in this case it's in your best interest to ask your editor: What are the chances you're actually going to commission this story? Is it scheduled?

Or you can get more direct: Is there any compensation involved in me researching this idea for you? We know freelancers who get research fees, so as much as editors are loath to talk about them, these fees are no surprise to them. Sometimes these are on top of the assignment, but more often, they're included in the eventual assignment's compensation. It pays to ask, especially if you're working with a new-to-you magazine.

Q&A

Q **What do I do if the editor offers me an "idea fee" for my story instead of an assignment?**

A An idea fee is a small payment — anywhere from $10 to $100 or more — the magazine gives the writer so the magazine can take the idea in-house. The magazine may use the idea for a reader survey, or assign it to a regular columnist. You get a little moolah — and zero credit. Idea fees are pesky things, but at least you can console yourself that the editor was honest enough to offer one to you instead of stealing the idea outright. Both Linda and Diana have been offered idea fees for stories, but if we needed a hand to count up the times this has happened, we could share one and leave the middle finger standing proud.

Idea fees tend to be offered for stories that are service-oriented or evergreen in nature: how to make your own ecologically correct teabags or the six steps to choosing your china pattern. If an idea fee isn't what you had in mind, there are ways to cope with — even profit from — the situation:

■ You can take the money and run — or better yet, use the experience to forge a bond with the editor. A sensitive editor will realize that an idea fee is a small consolation for the writer who was hoping for an assignment. Several years ago an editor at a parenting magazine apologetically offered Diana an idea fee, explaining it was something they wanted to use for a reader survey. Diana thought about the offer for 2.06 seconds and accepted the 50 bucks. She genuinely appreciated the editor's honesty and knew that by being agreeable, she'd be building up some good karma with the magazine. While the story idea was a good one, it was something of an evergreen — plus, she had tons more ideas to offer. Soon after, Diana sold the first of many stories to this editor.

■ Just say no. Especially if it's an idea you're passionate about and you're sure you can sell it elsewhere, there's no law that says you have to take the magazine's offer. If they're interested in it, there's probably another magazine that would be interested — and even better, willing to commission you to write it. You can thank the editor for the offer, and tell her your story isn't for sale. However, keep in mind there's no law preventing them from using the idea even if you say no to the fee — so do try to sell your story as fast as you can.

■ Talk to the editor before making a decision. Especially if his reason for the idea fee was vague, it can pay to weasel some information out of him. Give him a call, tell him you're curious about the offer, and see what he says. If he tells you they give big features like the one you've proposed only to writers they've worked with before, that's good information for you to work with. You could tell him you would prefer to write the story yourself and ask how you can convince him to give you the assignment. You could suggest working on a smaller story to prove yourself, for example, before they make a decision on the bigger piece. Perhaps a little bit of information from you is all they need to say, "Okay, how about we assign this as a department piece to you?" A little bit of chutzpah can take you way beyond a paltry idea fee.

Again, idea fees aren't the most horrible things you'll face as a freelancer. They're rare, and kind of a backhanded compliment to your awesome idea-generating power!

Q&A

Q My query got rejected. How do I follow up with the editor?

A There are different types of rejections. There's the bland, "Thanks but this doesn't quite meet our needs. Good luck placing it elsewhere" rejections, which we all hate receiving and that close the door to a meaningful response. Then there are other kinds of rejections, which aren't so much rejections but causes for celebration. We call them "nice rejections" and may you soon receive some!

Nice rejections are usually offered to a writer when an idea isn't quite right for the magazine, or the magazine already has something similar assigned to another writer, but the editor likes the writer's work enough to encourage him. These rejections usually include phrases like, "Feel free to pitch me more ideas," or "I like this idea, but it's not quite right," or "I'd like to see your clips." In short, you sense personality in the response, even if the encouragement doesn't fall into the effusive category. (Few editors heap effusive praise on writers — remember, at this point they're still wondering if you're the Lord Byron of freelancers — mad, bad, and dangerous to know.)

So if you've gotten one of these rejections, you must follow up. If you have one, send another idea immediately. You may begin your query, "Thank you for your encouraging response to my last story idea. Here's another idea I'd like to run by you." We have pitched and pitched to editors before getting an assignment, building a relationship with them along the way. For example, Diana pitched her editor at *Parenting* a dozen or so ideas before she landed her first feature assignment. A mailbox full of encouraging rejections didn't stop Diana from asking the editor if she wanted to meet the next time she was in New York. Not everyone can get to New York City easily, we know, but think about ways you can forge a bond with the editors who reject your pitches nicely.

What do I do if the editor rejected my idea but she asked me to send her more ideas — and I don't have any?

Yay! You've gotten one of those "nice rejections." Your query didn't hit the mark — perhaps they just assigned a similar idea to another writer, or the idea itself was a little off — but they want to hear more from you. Feel that love!

Okay, now the warm glow has burned off. You have a rejected query letter in your in-box and a growing feeling of panic. Now what do you do? This is when market-driven writers have the edge over idea-driven writers. An idea-driven writer is always hunting for markets to sell her ideas. If her idea doesn't pan out for one market, she's off to research another market where she can send it, so she simply may not have anything else appropriate to send to the editor. A market-driven writer, on the other hand, is always looking for ideas to sell to specific magazines. If the first idea she sends doesn't work out, she's usually got a few other story ideas at the ready.

Many of us fall into these categories without realizing it. If you've been sending out ideas willy nilly and gotten anxious when editors encourage you to send more ideas, you may want to think about becoming more market-driven in your querying efforts. Are there certain magazines you want to crack? What kinds of stories would you like to write for these magazines? Do you have a list of possible story ideas that would work for them? If not, start building that list today so you don't get caught short the next time you query.

Say you've already gotten yourself into a pickle: an editor at Magazine A, a magazine you really, really want to write for, rejected your pitch on a breaking development in dermatitis control, but she encouraged you to send more ideas. If you're lucky, she may have given you some direction ("Our beauty editor handles skin stories in house, but we are looking for more women's reproductive health stories"), in which case your job is much easier. You can take a look through a few back issues, see what they've done with women's reproductive health, and run with it. A vague "feel free to pitch me" is a little trickier when you feel like you don't have anything appropriate to send. Diana has had some luck shooting off a friendly e-mail to these editors, thanking them for their encouraging response and asking if there's anything specific they're looking for in future pitches so she can hit the target. Some editors don't respond, but others have kindly provided everything from a short directive ("We need age 0-1 baby development stories") to a laundry list of wants. There's no guarantee you'll get either, but why not try?

Needless to say, you should also spend some time studying back issues of the magazine, if you haven't already. Are they publishing more "as-told-to" women's health stories? Think about some women you know whose medical conditions might make great articles. Do recent issues seem to have more quizzes written by freelancers? Does each story have a celebrity link? As you're flipping through and taking notes, keep asking yourself, "How can I contribute?"

What paralyzes many writers when they get an encouraging rejection is that they think they have to respond to the editor quickly, or else the connection will be lost. Sure, it's great if you can strike while the iron's hot, but if you don't have anything to send to the editor, don't let panic set in. Better to come up with an idea she'll actually want to buy a month later, than to send some half-assed query for the sake of timeliness or to convince yourself you have nothing else to send and walk away. Besides, no editor is sitting at her desk, spasmodically checking her e-mail for a new query from you. When you finally do come up with some ideas that are right for her, paste her "nice rejection" into the body of your new e-mail, warmly thank her for her encouraging response, and pitch away.

QIs it okay to pitch a story over the phone?

AThere are indeed times when you should not write a query letter and instead pitch your story by phone. You can let your fingers do the walking and your mouth do the talking when:

■ The story is so timely that a few days delay could kill it.

■ You have an established relationship with the editor and you want to gauge interest in a story before working on a proposal.

■ You're pitching a newspaper. Newspaper editors often appreciate phone pitches because they can say yea or nay and move on without a paper trail.

If you're glib on the phone, you can push the envelope with these guidelines. If you're leaving on a trip to a remote part of Nepal to altitude train with Sherpas, you could try calling editors at adventure magazines, if only to prime them for a query you'll write when you get back. Who knows? Maybe they had a story meeting that morning and someone mourned aloud, "I wish we had a writer in Nepal." Stranger things have happened.

Keep your phone pitches brief and to the point. Start your spiel by asking if it's a good time to talk (naturally, many people will say, "Well, no, it's not," which is when you say, "Then I'll keep this short. I'm a writer who's traveling to Nepal next week ....") If you have built up a good relationship with an editor, ask if you can call during a scheduled time with some story ideas. Many editors are especially receptive to these kinds of calls — they can make quick decisions on the phone without having to take any followup action. You benefit by not wasting time on stories he wouldn't consider.

Use the telephone judiciously and wisely and you can pave the way to a great assignment.

Q Do I have to send in a query for an essay?

A In a word, no. Editors generally prefer to read a finished essay, since so much of this writing is driven by the essayist's voice. Remember your fifth-grade teacher exhorting you to "show, don't tell" in your writing? A query letter that assures an editor your essay is "funny, uplifting, and touches the human spirit" tells, not shows. Better to let editors judge for themselves how funny your writing is or how the story of your grandmother's prizewinning crocheted afghan lifts the heart and spirit.

If you plan on sending your essay by e-mail, include it in the body of your e-mail, not as an attachment. All you need is a short "cover note" to introduce your essay. Start with a salutation ("Dear Mr. Smith"), and then briefly introduce yourself and background ("My essays have been published in *Salon*, *The Washington Post*, and *Guideposts*."). Wrap up your cover note with a date you'd like to hear back (if it's a time-sensitive essay), and how the editor can contact you. That's it!

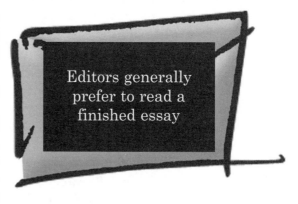

Editors generally prefer to read a finished essay

QDo I have to write a query for a short department piece?

A We know — it seems ludicrous to write a 1,000-word query for a story that might run at 1/10th that length. Many writers we know don't bother with the query letter at all: they write up the short piece and send it in. This can be a good strategy if you have all the research and reporting finished — for example, a short piece on a unique hotel in San Francisco where you rented a pet for your stay.

If, on the other hand, you'll need to interview an author or track down studies to write the piece, it may be better to query first. Keep the query short — here is where editors will definitely be interested in seeing how tight you can write. Maybe give them one or two sentences written in the flavor of the magazine, a couple sentences about how you'll approach the piece or the questions you'll answer, then end with a sentence or two about yourself. That's it.

If you've written for the magazine before, you can often pitch a bunch of these ideas in a bulleted list form. Your editor already knows you've got the chops to get the story and write it efficiently, so there's no need to go into a lot of detail.

Q&A

Q Is it okay to pitch a business magazine a story about my best friend's new Internet venture?

A Yes — to another journalist. Sorry, but it's lousy journalistic practice to pitch stories about family members' and friends' businesses to your editors. For one thing, journalists are supposed to be unbiased. Even if you feel you can write the story fairly, the appearance of bias is enough to make your editors cringe. The only time it's okay to use a family member or friend as a source is perhaps in a story where it's clear they're your relative or friend. For example, a parenting magazine would probably be okay with, "One day when I was talking to my sister-in-law about temper tantrums, she said ...." It's also okay if the relationship is central to the theme of the article. For example, for an article on snoring, it would be fine to say in your lede how your wife's zzzzzs drive you to another resting place at night. (Your wife might not be fine with this, but that's another book.)

An ethical journalist will pass on the story. An ethical and nice journalist will pass the story on to another journalist who can report and write fairly and without bias. An ethical, nice, and busy journalist has too many other great stories to get her knickers in a twist about this "lost" opportunity.

Q If I want to pitch travel stories, should I go on my trip first, or pitch before I depart?

A This comes down to personal preference — there's no right or wrong. Many travel writers prefer to line up assignments before they leave for Moscow or the Outer Hebrides — that way they can plan their itineraries efficiently and know what they'll need to do once they step off the plane. Assignments in hand may give them credibility with foreign agencies or tourism bureaus, or access to hard-to-get sources. If they run into roadblocks during reporting, they can check in with an assigning editor to get advice or clarification. On top of all this, they know there are some checks forthcoming to cover the cost of the trip. The downside to a super-structured trip is that you may pass by really good stories you hadn't planned for — a side excursion to a remote island inhabited by rare two-headed frogs you have to shelve because you're scheduled for hard-to-land local interviews that day.

Other writers need to get the feel of a place before they can pitch. They hop on a plane with an open mind — and an open wallet — and look for angles and stories that grab them. They'll write up these ideas and send them when they're on the road, or do all their reporting and wait to get home to write everything up. Sometimes they'll even call editors while they're in the place and pitch over the phone. The downside of the travel-then-pitch strategy is there's no guarantee you'll be able to place stories when you get home. If income is an issue for you — and it is for most of the hardworking freelancers we know — it's going to be a bitter pill if your $5,000 trip to Las Vegas results only in a $50 short for a local newspaper. (And best of luck slipping that trip by the IRS!)

The smart answer seems to be to do a little of both: pitch before traveling, then pitch again when you're home. If you're heading off to distant lands with a knapsack stuffed with assignments, leave some room in your schedule to take advantage of chance opportunities and sudden adventures. If you prefer writing when you get home, at least give it the old college try to get some interest in your trip from editors — at least you'll have them primed and ready for your pitches when you come home.

Q Should I mention in my query letter that I got this story through a press trip or that my hotel expenses were comped by a tourism board?

A Some newspapers and magazines are very, very strict about press trips and comps. (Comps are the freebies the travel industry heaps on editors and writers — free stays at resorts, no-charge five-course dinners at Michelin-rated restaurants, etc.) These policies are in place to assure readers that the writer's opinions are not compromised. To write for these publications, writers either have to pay their travel costs out of pocket, or wait for an assignment where the magazine or newspaper covers expenses.

Some travel writers adopt a policy of "don't ask/don't tell." They feel how they got their story is no one's business but their own. There are many magazines and newspapers that don't have policies on comped trips — or they leave it up to the writer to enforce his own ethical guidelines. Writers in the "don't ask/don't tell" camp send their pitches out to target magazines and hope that if the story is accepted, the question doesn't come up. (Again, with a great number of magazines, it doesn't.) Obviously, they don't spill the beans in their query letters, either. We know several journalists who cover travel and who regularly go on press junkets — they know which magazines and newspapers will welcome their stories, and they avoid the places with strict rules.

We advise writers to respect the magazines and newspapers with rules. It's not very smart (or ethical) to go on a press trip, then sign a statement swearing you didn't go on one. Travel writers and editors are a tight bunch — you may find out the hard way that your editor at *The Journal of Ethical Travel* is good friends with the travel editor at *Swag Times,* who did comped tequila shots with you in a comped hotel suite down in Anguilla … first-class flight comped, of course. Word gets around fast in these circles.

If you query a magazine with a strict policy on press trips or media comps, it's probably a selling point to mention in your letter that your travel expenses were paid out of pocket, if indeed they were. You don't have to bang the editor over the head with it. Just say something like, "I was in Rome on a family vacation when I discovered one of Italy's best kept secrets, Maria's Gelateria."

Q Will I always have to write query letters?

A We know a lot of writers who hate querying — but honestly, it's hands down our favorite part of freelancing (besides cashing checks, that is). Okay, so you're ready to shoot spitballs into our hair-do's for admitting that. Well, take solace, friend — once you've gotten in the door of a few magazines, you'll find that you won't always have to query for assignments. And even if you do, you won't have to sweat as hard over your letters. Here's why:

Once you've turned in a couple of articles to a magazine, you'll become a known quantity to your editor. You turn assignments in on time. Your writing is clean. You don't bitch and moan when she asks you to do a rewrite. Your ideas become more targeted because you start seeing what works and what doesn't for the magazine. And your editor likes you, she really likes you. One day you might get an e-mail from her asking if you have any ideas to help her fill a section. She might call you with a rush assignment. She may even start calling you with her own ideas. You have arrived at a place where querying isn't as important anymore.

Of course, many magazine editors love it when writers come to them with great stories. But if querying is something you loathe, take comfort in the fact that you'll probably do less of it once you're established. Until then, think of querying as part of paying your dues.

Q&A

How many query letters should I have circulating? How many should I get out per week?

There's no golden number we can give you. We tell beginning writers it's better to have three extremely well-written and targeted queries in circulation than a dozen half-baked proposals that make editors wonder, "Who is this nincompoop and why is he writing to me?" Learning how to write a good sales letter is hard work — so spend your salad days learning how to do this well versus doing it fast.

At some point in your career — for some writers this comes at three months, for others, three years — the whole process of writing a query letter will start to click. You develop a style that works for you. You have a better idea of what resonates with editors and know how to write a lede that grabs attention. What used to take you days to write now takes you a few hours. Sometimes — hallelujah! — you write query letters in a matter of minutes and sell them in a day. Work is starting to trickle in, and you even have repeat business. You have arrived!

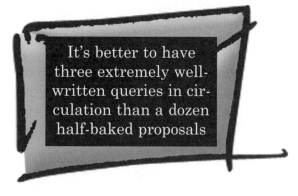

It's better to have three extremely well-written queries in circulation than a dozen half-baked proposals

Now's the time to think about a query quota. We hope you're keeping track of queries and noticing how many sell versus how many don't. Some writers use math to come up with a formula. For example, say you're averaging ten queries out the door each month. Out of those ten queries, two produce sales. If you're comfortable with making two sales per month, than you can aim for keeping ten queries in circulation. If you'd like to make four sales per month, you should get 20 queries circulating, keeping in mind that your batting average may get better down the road. (Yes, you can get too good at querying and end up with too much work on your plate.)

Query Letters that Rock

Some writers have such a hard time writing queries that they give themselves a weekly quota not based on sales, and that's okay, too. Just keep the quota reasonable. Set yourself up for success by telling yourself you'll get one query out this week, and shoot for two next week. If one gets rejected, you can get it right back out the door to another editor and count it toward your quota.

When Diana was starting out she had a weekly query quota. Although she loves querying today, in the beginning it wasn't so much fun, so she rewarded herself every time she hit the send button. Each query earned her a frozen Snickers ice cream bar. If she made her quota for the week, she got her favorite Starbucks coffee drink, plus a book. Eventually she gave up the rewards system, because she got so good at querying that her backside expanded from the volume of chocolate and sweetened coffee drinks she ingested.

Q&A

Q **Should I buy query writing software to give me an edge?**

A Hey, we're all about saving time when it comes to writing queries, so we checked out a Web site that sells "Instant Query Letter Software." The word "instant" really appealed to us, because we don't want to spend even one second working when we could be out striking fear into the hearts of baristas everywhere.

The site had pages of super-hyped sales-talk with words underlined, bold, and in different colors. It's a scientifically proven fact that if a Web site makes you want to don sunglasses, the product must be good! And what if, as the site reads, "just one article of yours got published in a huge magazine that made you famous virtually overnight..."? Sign us up!

But we started cluing in to the red flags when the software creator called herself "Jane Doe, Successful Author (of way too many publications to list here)." Hmmm ... so you can take several scrolled-down pages to tout the wonderfulness of your software, but you can't spare the space to list your creds?

We did a little research online. A Google search showed no publications by this author. Amazon.com turned up no books under that author's name. Findarticles.com found no articles. The only thing we could find, in fact, were e-books that the author was selling through her own site. We could be wrong — after all, not every writer is like us, bragging about her creds to all and sundry — but it seems that if you're a writer with "too many publications to list," people should be able to find your books and articles online.

But we were still enticed by the prospect of pressing a button and getting, "like magic," a "highly professional, completely irresistible query letter." Besides, we can't give the author's lack of credentials too much weight — perhaps she is actually a shy, reclusive soul, and writes under pseudonyms like "Susan Orlean" and "Dan Brown." So we shelled out 37 bucks to try out the instant query letter software.

Here's the scoop. Sit down and get out your pen, for you are about to become rich and famous!

Query Letters that Rock

In short, you're asked to fill in fields with info like your name, the editor's name, the magazine and address, your credentials, the target market, a word count, rights offered, and — hey, what's this? — an opening statement, a description of your article, and a statement about what the reader will learn from your article. This is a far cry from the "magic" we were promised. Where is the fairy dust? Where are the elves? Where's David Copperfield?

(To be fair, the software isn't totally unhelpful: Under each field are useful tips that include such gems as "Be creative! Grab attention!" and "... make sure this is correctly spelled!")

After filling in all the fields, you press a button and — wait for it — the software generates a query that cobbles together all the information you put into it, with a couple of bits thrown in to connect it all together.

So, in sum, you are paying $37 for the rare and unique opportunity to write your own query letter, and not a very good one at that. What you put in goes out. If you suck, your query sucks. Even if what you put in doesn't suck, the form leaves no room to really flesh out the idea with quotes and examples, and it certainly doesn't give you much of a chance to show your voice.

We're now $37 poorer, but hey, we live (and shell out the smackers) in service to our readers. Want to show us your appreciation? Send us the 37 bucks — we'll probably be grateful enough to share a secret that's actually worth something.

Q&A

Q **How can I prevent an editor from stealing my idea?**

A You might as well ask, "How can I keep liars out of government?" Editors would have us believe that story poaching from freelancers never happens — that every idea we pitch to them has been heard before, that there is nothing new under the sun, blah blah blah. But hey, we'd be remiss in our Renegade Writer duties to accept an editor's word on this important subject. Idea theft does happen. It has happened to both of us. The good news is it happens very rarely — more rarely than timely payment from a magazine! And while there are a few things you can do to prevent theft from happening, particularly wily thieves will always figure out a way to pilfer and plunder from hapless writers.

For example, a couple of years ago Diana pitched a profile subject to a women's magazine editor. The editor pounced on the idea, asking Diana dozens of questions over a period of several months about the woman, everything from how old she was to what her two adult daughters did for a living. Answering her questions took several interviews, plus hours of research time.

Then the source called and told Diana that a contributing editor (CE) from the magazine had called to schedule an interview. The CE had explained to her that the source's name had come up during a magazine meeting — and the source wanted to know if was a problem if she talked to the CE? Before Diana could say "Yes, big problem!" Diana's editor sent her a short e-mail: " Unbeknownst to me, another editor has already included (and interviewed) [source's name] in a larger … feature we are doing for the magazine. We simply cannot use her in two stories. I'm sorry—she really was the perfect [subject]! Thanks so much for all the research and effort you put into pitching me this story." (Obviously perfect enough to hand to the CE for her story.) Diana was furious at the cavalier attitude the editor had with her profile subject and vowed never to work with her again.

The problem with query letters and proposals is that they require a lot of information that can be picked over and looted by a less-than-ethical editor: everything from sources (as in Diana's case) to facts and figures. Usually idea thieves at the editorial level steal bits and pieces, rather than nabbing the whole pie. For example, they won't five-finger your feature idea on yoga, but they'll lift the research you've uncovered for a story they're writing in-house. You get a rejection note as a thank you.

So now we've got you cowering the corner. Please, come on out. Again, this kind of stuff rarely happens. Also, there are a few things you can do to protect yourself. First, if this is a story where a source figures prominently, prior to sending your proposal you can ask your source to promise he won't speak to anyone else but you. If the magazine contacts him on the sly, you'll soon find out about it.

Second, hold back some cards in your query. This can be a little tricky. If you've got some great quotes for a hard-to-report story,

> If you've got some great quotes for a hard-to-report story, give only the source's name

for example, give only the source's name, but not her city and state, so she can't be hunted down by the magazine. If you quote a renowned plastic surgeon, rather than give her name, you can quote her as "a prominent Fifth Avenue plastic surgeon I interviewed for this story." The third strategy goes against what we say above: write your queries so they're as identifiable as your fingerprints. Says Kristin Godsey, editor of *Writer's Digest*, "I think the more information you put in your query, the less likely an editor is to steal it — after all, if the article appears in the magazine and makes all the same points you made in your query, quoting the exact experts you'd said you'd talk to, then you've got a strong argument to prove your claim that you were ripped off (and then get compensation)."

Providing too little info can hurt you in other ways, too. "The failure to provide enough information in a query is a common problem we see at our magazine," says Ron Kovach, senior editor at

Q&A

The Writer. "We've even coined a term for it: 'keeping the editor in suspense.' A typical example is a writer proposing to provide, say, seven tips on how to get past writer's block and then not telling us what any of her tips are. This happens more often than you'd guess. It's quite annoying and time-consuming, because if an editor is at all interested in a query, then he or she is forced to e-mail the writer for additional information that should have been provided in the first place. I'm sure there are many editors who aren't that patient and will reject such a vague query on the spot."

Many writers will squawk, "Thief, thief!" but when you look at their queries, they're either evergreens ("How to toilet train your toddler in a week") or vague enough to seem similar ("Yoga: The latest research"). Before you approach the magazine with your claim, really examine the alleged breach. Get the opinions of trusted colleagues. Accusing someone of theft is a serious allegation that you need to prove beyond a reasonable doubt. In the rare cases where our ideas were lifted, we simply walked away from the editor and magazine, vowing never to work with them again and spreading the word to other writers about their nasty habits. There are enough professional and ethical editors out there to keep us busy.

Q Ooops. I just found a mistake in my query letter. What should I do?

A Even if you've proofread your query letter dozens of times, the occasional boo-boo sometimes sneaks through. It happens to the best of us. We make boo-boos all the time — tiny things like forgetting an end parenthesis or dropping a word like "to" out of a sentence — and still end up selling the queries. We do spell check and all that, but sometimes those annoying little errors persist in their evil ways. So if you find one (or two) after you hit send, cross your fingers, say a Hail Mary and hope your editor doesn't notice.

As we toil and sweat over writing query letters, we imagine our editors giving them the same level of focused attention. The reality is that most editors have only thirty seconds or less to give your letter a read. If the writing is extraordinary, she might slow down as her enthusiasm builds. She may notice a tiny typo or a missing punctuation mark, but if the rest of the query letter enchants, she'll fast forget your faux pas. Even better are your chances that she won't notice it at all.

Repeat to yourself: everyone makes mistakes

Bigger boo-boos are when you spell an editor's name wrong or mix up magazine names. Again, nearly every professional writer has made this kind of error. (Linda recently wrote to an editor named "Gay" and called her "Gey"!) We won't kid you — those kind of errors hurt because they usually do get noticed and remarked upon, either with a rejection or a straight-out admonishment to get it right next time.

If it's a tiny error, let it go. Even if you've misspelled the name of an expert source you plan to interview, pray that the editor hasn't heard of him and fix it next time you send the query out or when you're completing the assignment. A bigger error, like misspelling the editor's name? If you've just hit send and noticed the error, you can correct it right away and resend it with a short explanation and apology.

Repeat to yourself: everyone makes mistakes. Focus more on not making the same mistakes over and over, and you'll be a happier writer. If you're slipping too many typos or silly punctuation errors into your queries, think about ways you can improve the quality of your work: maybe take a proofreading course through a continuing education program or hire your unemployed English major sister to give your queries and articles a glance.

Section II: Query Letters That Rock!

Ready to ride the magic carpet into the strange, unfamiliar kingdom called an editor's brain? In this section, you'll find query letters that rocked an editor's socks off — and better yet, we strongarmed the editors into telling us why these letters led them to commission the article. We also talked to the writers to learn how they put their pitch together. Ready for transport? Takeoff!

Women's Health

It's not often that an editor is hit with an idea that makes her sit up and take notice — but that's what happened when Julia Rosien combined two unexpected topics: pregnancy and sex. Start your query with a lede that shocks the editor and makes her want to keep reading, which Julia did by starting off with a shocking anecdote from a source. (Of course, she backs up all this surprising stuff with solid research.)

Dear Leah:

Lori didn't catch wind of her first orgasm until she was thirty — and pregnant. "I could never find that last sweet spot, no matter how hard I tried." She's not alone. According to the Journal of the American Medical Association, 70 percent of women don't have orgasms during intercourse, and 30 percent miss out completely.

All right, the truth. Pregnancy isn't likely to conjure images of a sexual free-for-all. We know it's shocking, but good old-fashioned athletic sex isn't topic number one in most of those baby manuals stacked beside your bed. Consider this: a pregnant woman's body increases blood flow by one third, and blood vessels dilate quicker and with less stimulation. "Unless there is a specific high risk situation where the MD warns the couple against it, there is no reason why pregnant sex life, including intercourse, can't be as juicy as ever — even juicier," says Dr. Shoshana S. Bennett, Ph.D., perinatal specialist and author of Beyond the Blues.

With the help of experts (as well as the first-hand knowledge from my own four pregnancies) I'd love to share some knocked-up sexual knowledge with your readers. "A Field Guide to Great

Pregnant Sex" will explore the exciting sexual changes, as well as some common misconceptions about sex during pregnancy. I'll interview experts in the field and delve into the different options (and positions) that make pregnant sex the best sex ever. Possible sidebars could include information on when sex isn't fun during pregnancy. It sounds like shutting the barn door after the horse has escaped, but falling out of sync sexually during pregnancy isn't uncommon. While I estimate a word length of 2000 words for this story, that's flexible depending on your editorial needs.

I'm a senior editor at ePregnancy Magazine, an international monthly consumer magazine. As well, I'm a freelancer who's contributed to publications including Wedding Style, The Christian Science Monitor and CBC Radio. I also hold memberships at various professional organizations, including the Professional Writer's Association of Canada (PWAC).

Please let me know if you have questions about this story idea. I'll be happy to fax or email you samples of my writing. Thanks for your time; I look forward to hearing from you soon!

Yours,
Julia Rosien

The Writer: **Julia Rosien**

I was looking for a way to use some of my expertise to get into new markets. I do a lot of pregnancy writing, and I thought this was an unusual topic that I hadn't seen covered before. I look for things you haven't seen in every magazine. I wanted to write about sex during pregnancy with honesty, and to give all the details readers need. It's a pretty edgy topic and I knew that *Women's Health* isn't afraid of tackling those topics.

I've never had any trouble finding experts for my queries. I just approach the expert professionally and say I'd like to write an article about X. I don't mention who I'm writing for, but if the source asks where the article is to be published, I'm frank with them and tell them I'm in the query stages and I hope to get it placed in Y magazine. New writers get nervous about how to approach an expert, but it's in your own head. It's not something most experts are concerned with. They're happy to talk because they know the potential of being mentioned in a magazine is far greater if they're helpful.

To get the women-on-the-street quote, I went trolling on different discussion boards online where pregnant women post questions. It's amazing how many people are willing to talk about their sex life. Because it's e-mail, there's that computer screen between you and the interviewer that makes it easier to open up.

I didn't put her quote in the article itself because she wouldn't give me permission to use her last name. But all of my expert advice pointed to the fact that what she had said is statistically true. It's a touchy topic for someone to allow their first and last name to appear in a magazine.

I offer sidebars with every query I write, even if it's just a FOB [Front-Of-the-Book, which refers to the short, quick-read articles at the beginning of many magazines]. Sometimes the editor doesn't like the article idea, but the sidebar sounds interesting so we have a discussion about that. I always offer a little bit more so there's room to negotiate.

I always include a proposed word count — and it never is the word count the editor wants. For this article I had proposed 2,000 words but ended up writing 700 words. But it shows that you have an image of what you want to write and have a plan in place. The word count doesn't help the editors as much as it helps me; I have a visual image of what I want to write and how it's going to look. If the editor comes back and says, "I can use 700 words, would you be willing to do that?" I can reformulate the plan in my own mind.

Looking back on it, I think the query was too wordy, but I was proposing a 2,000 word article. I don't think it's a detriment to the writer if the query is long but really well written.

As an editor, I'd like to tell writers to always include contact information. It's amazing how many writers will sign with their name and e-mail, and I have no idea who they are or where they live. Even though it's e-mail, projecting an aura of professionalism lets an editor know you're serious and will follow through what you've promised in your query.

The Editor: Leah Flickinger, Senior Editor

The first line really grabbed me ... it was really compelling. I do see a lot of sex and relationship stuff, and this was counterintuitive in a way. You don't hear so much about women who hit 30 who haven't had an orgasm. And the fact that she was pregnant — women have so many different feelings about sex during pregnancy; it's such a loaded issue.

Ultimately we went back and forth on structure and format. Julia had pitched it as a much longer story and we decided we couldn't do as many words. We have FOB opportunities for shorter pieces. Our readers' average age is 31, and most are married or in a committed relationship. Some of them have small children, but not all of them. So pregnancy sex is something we wouldn't necessarily want to devote too many pages to.

It didn't bother me that she gave a word length. All it took was one e-mail asking if she'd be willing to do fewer words. And she was perfectly willing. If you're going to put a word length in a query, it might make sense to say, "I estimate X words, but that's flexible."

Including a proposed title is good because it ties the idea up with a nice bow. You want to be concise in a query, but if you have a couple of title ideas, it may not be a bad idea to put them both down.

Writers often do quote experts in their query, which I think is fine, but I don't think it's necessary. However, I do like to have an idea of what kind of experts a writer will talk to. I know a lot of experts in the sex and relationships area, and some are used over and over, so I like to see new ones. Also, I like to be confident that the writer is not going to be relying on their own OBGYN or the local doctor next door. You want the most qualified expert for the topic, maybe someone who's done research or written a book in addition to having a practice.

AARP: The Magazine

Got connections? Use 'em! If you've met an editor at a conference, online, or even at the local coffee shop, remind him of your cosmic connection. This query is also a study in slanting your specialty in unexpected ways to fit all kinds of markets. Who would have thought that a magazine aimed at people over 50 would run a piece about video games? Writer Damon Brown did, and he scored not one, but two assignments.

Hi Mr. Budd,

This is freelance writer Damon Brown; we had dinner during the One-on-One Conference here in Chicago. How have you been? I hope all is well.

We spoke about my Nintendo-loving grandfather and how a significant percentage of video game players are now over the age of 45. International Digital Software Association President Douglas Lowenstein recently said that older people were part of the new gamer profile, and recent evidence shows that he's not too far from the truth.

A 2004 study found that 37 percent of 45 to 54 year olds and 26 percent of 55 to 64 year olds plan on buying at least one video game this year. Furthermore, the nearly-octogenarian Hugh Hefner is releasing Playboy: The Mansion, a role playing game where you get to play the magazine mogul and get him out of special...situations. Obviously, the gaming audience has grown up.

I would like to do a Navigator piece on this growing trend of game playing older folks. I will discuss the Playboy game and other titles geared towards people over 45. I will contact the Entertainment Software Association and learn more about the burgeoning demographic. I will also talk with KY Enterprises, which specializes in video game controllers for the disabled and elderly.

I cover technology and pop culture for Playboy.com, MSN.com, Electronic Gaming Monthly and other publications. I have my Masters in Magazine Publishing from Northwestern University.

Below are links to my online portfolio and two clips. The first piece, from the music magazine The Source, is an investigative piece on how African-Americans are portrayed in video games. The second article, from the Journal of the American Dietetic Association, is a lead feature on the boom in fortified drinks, such as Propel and Vitamin Water. Feel free to contact me if you would like more articles.

Thanks and take care!
Damon Brown

The Writer: **Damon Brown**

When I was growing up, I used to spend summers with my grandparents and cousins in New Jersey. My granddad was a very nice guy, but extremely quiet; I'd ask a million questions and he'd have one-word answers. I wasn't sure how to connect with him. When the Nintendo Entertainment System came out in 1986, my grandfather got one. Almost every day I'd play video games with him, and we'd talk about games and we'd talk a little about life. My family and I had left New Jersey a few years prior, but the Nintendo was one of the ways that my granddad and I would stay connected.

When I went to the One-On-One conference in Chicago, a conference where writers get to pitch ideas to magazine editors, I thought there would be nothing I could pitch to *AARP* magazine. I'm not even 30 yet, so how could I contribute to the lives of people over 50? But that evening in the shower I remembered playing video games with my grandfather and wondered how many other older people played video games.

When I met with Ken Budd from *AARP*, I told him about my

grandfather. He asked if I had any evidence of video game playing being a trend among older people. I wasn't sure at the time, but I had the resources to find out. Mr. Budd said that if I could find the statistics, we could do this.

Two months later I followed up with some solid facts, and he said this was one of his favorite queries that he got from the conference.

I think it helped to start the query with a personal connection. In fact, since they had two dinner nights during the course of the One-On-One, I ended up having dinner with Mr. Budd before I even had anything to pitch. It's one of those cases where you never know who you might be working with in the future. That's why I think it's important to cultivate relationships.

I got the stats for my query from a speech by Douglas Lowenstein, president of the International Digital Software Association. I occasionally do interviews for queries, but usually I don't.

One of my advantages is that I have three specialties: video games, sex, and music. Almost everything I write has to do with those three things or an overlap of them. When I approached Mr. Budd about the article, I already knew who I could talk to, as I had a few established contacts. That made it easier for me to do the query, but also for the people I contacted to understand that I respected their field. When you have a certain specialty, it makes it easier to get into special interest publications.

I didn't include any clips with the query. A colleague of mine who was just starting out built a Web site for me pro bono. The site has an uploadable database where I can upload new articles as I pub-lish them. Now when I send a query, particularly for the publica-tions that are high up there and very busy, I can just send them links to my articles. If they're interested, they can click on them. Response time has been quicker, and I haven't had one magazine that has asked me for hard copy clips. Magazines are becoming more tech savvy, and a lot of editors just don't have whole lot of time. Sometimes they don't even have a chance to read hard copy clips, so I think it helps to have clips online.

Query Letters that Rock

The Editor: Ken Budd, Features Editor

Damon started by mentioning that we'd discussed his idea at the One-On-One conference. Good idea to refresh my memory — I met with a lot of writers that weekend — though he probably should have reminded me why I liked the idea. We get bombarded with queries, so you need to make yours stand out.

Like most editors, I want to be surprised. A lot of the queries we get are on topics we've already done or ideas that aren't new to us. One way to separate yourself from the crowd: Take advantage of any inside connection. I know of at least one proposal that got my attention (and ultimately a sale) because the pitch noted that a writer I use frequently thought it would be right for the magazine.

Damon's idea is exactly the kind of thing we're looking for: it's surprising, counterintuitive, and I hadn't seen it covered anywhere else (it's always a turnoff to get pitched on an idea that appeared in that day's *New York Times*). The natural assumption is that video gamers are all geeky fourteen-year-old boys — not folks in their fifties. Ideally, however, the query would have gone a step further (something the story ultimately did) by showing that 50+ Americans aren't just playing video games, they're excelling at them. Aside from his grandfather, he doesn't include any examples of game-obsessed people over 50.

I like that Damon included statistics; it shows that he's done some digging and can support his idea as a trend. With a lot of queries it's hard to know if the person is qualified to write the story. Celebrity interviews are a good example. Writers say, "Hey, I'd like to interview Paul Newman." Okay, but do you have an inside connection with him or his agent? Have you covered the film industry? What makes you the right person for this piece?

The writing style of this query is pretty straightforward, which is fine since we'd already talked about the idea. Typically, however, I prefer queries that are gripping right from the opening sentence. Every editor here gets stacks of queries, which means you typically look at the first paragraph, and if it isn't a grabber, you move on. If your query is dull, why should the story be any different?

You should always play to your strengths in your query. Damon may not have had an overwhelming number of credits, but he showed that he knows his subject. Also, since this is the front-of-the-book piece, we'll take a chance on new-to-us writers.

This was a double sale for Damon: He got the Navigator [a department] piece and also a Web-exclusive piece on the best video games for people over 50. You should be thinking of not just a story, but also a Web offshoot, sidebars, or stories for different versions of our magazine. We do three editions targeted to different age groups. If you say something about writing for our older edition, it says to me that you've been studying the magazine.

By mentioning this company that develops products for older Americans, Damon showed that he's targeting the story to our audience. A lot of pitches we receive are for stories that could appear in any magazine, not one for readers age 50 and older.

American Baby

If you've had a rotten experience, take solace in the fact that it may boost your bank account — once you turn it into a salable article idea. Some of the best ideas come from personal experience, and many writers who are parents find that their kids provide a wellspring of topics.

This writer went way long with her query, and it paid off. The editor was impressed that the writer included all the information she'd need to envision the article in her magazine, including a title, a sidebar idea, anecdotes, and quotes.

Also, this writer bucked the system by e-mailing her query even though she had been told to send it via snail mail. Long live the Renegade Writer revolution!

Dear Ms. Porretta,

It was 3 a.m., and my 9-month-old daughter, Mira, had been throwing up for the better part of the night. My husband called his sister, a veteran mom of two kids. "It's a stomach bug," she said. "You just have to ride it out." She recommended small sips of Pedialyte every 20 minutes.

Thinking there must be something else that would make that "Mommy, why can't you make it better?" look leave my baby's eyes, I called the doctor.

After hearing the symptoms, the doctor-on-call, a stranger to me, asked just two questions — Mira's age and our insurance carrier — before making his pronouncement: "Go to the emergency room."

When the ER doctors told us to do exactly what my sister-in-law had advised, I was a bit ashamed. How much time had we wasted waiting in the ER? How much more comfortable would my child have been at home? When we saw the bill — $975 — I had to wonder how people like us played into rising health care costs.

This was not the first time my doctor had told me to go to the ER for a minor ailment, usually on a Friday night when there were no office hours until Monday. In fact, 46 percent of patients under age 18 who went to the ER sought non-urgent care, according to the February issue of Pediatric Emergency Care. Children ages 1-4 were the most commonly treated group.

My article, "Crying Wolf: Is the ER really necessary?" will inform readers why a doctor would recommend an emergency room visit, how to talk to your pediatrician to ensure that such a step is truly necessary, and what to do when your child is hurting and you are panicked.

Some pediatricians are making changes to help stem the ER tide. At a practice in Howell, Mich., patients know they can get same-day appointments. Sick on a Saturday? The doctor is in. And if it's the middle of the night and a high fever is causing concern, you will talk to a doctor from your practice, someone you know and who knows you and your child, says medical director Dr. April Joy Ping.

"By calling us, we can help differentiate the really bad from the not-so-bad," said Dr. Ping. "When you know the patient, you are more comfortable assessing what they are telling you."

Brendan McKillip, a suburban Chicago father, didn't even think of calling the pediatrician when his 2-1/2-year-old daughter howled in pain over an injured wrist. It was the weekend, after all, and he admits now that his was a panicked response.

"Looking back we would have considered the situation a bit more thoroughly," says McKillip. His daughter's reaction was more a result of her being tired, not injured. Had he thought out the situation, and called his pediatrician first, he could have saved his family the ER wait. His daughter wouldn't have had to undergo unnecessary medical tests. And he would have saved on his insurance co-pay for ER visits.

My article, "Crying Wolf," would include a sidebar on what information parents should have on hand when they call the doctor, such as an accurate temperature.

In addition to Dr. Ping, I will speak with Dr. Karen Zimmer of Johns Hopkins Hospital, Bethesda, Md., who authored the Pediatric Emergency Care journal article. I will also include other ER stories from real parents.

I am a medical writer with 10 years of reporting experience. I served as health editor at The Monroe Evening News in Monroe, Mich. for six years and also specialized in parenting and lifestyle feature writing. Examples of my work are available at www.cynthiaramnarace.com.

I look forward to discussing "Crying Wolf: Is the ER really necessary?" with you further.

Sincerely,
Cynthia Ramnarace

The Writer: Cynthia Ramnarace

I came up with this idea when my daughter got sick in April 2005. We were sitting in the emergency room and I was getting ticked off at the whole process and the idea came from there. I saw that *Parenting* had just had an article about emergency room visits, though it wasn't the same spin. I was a bit apprehensive about querying *Parents* since they're so huge. So *American Baby* was the first magazine I sent the query off to.

You can't trust mastheads to find out who the correct editor is to pitch, so I just called the magazine. I reached an editorial assistant and described my idea, and she said to send it to Christine. She said to send the query by mail, so I did some cyber-stalking and found Christine's e-mail address.

I started out with a personal anecdote. I would definitely do that with all the parenting magazines because so many of them are first person-centric. Coming from a newspaper background, I had to rethink the way I do things; in newspapers, you take yourself out of the reporting. So putting myself into it is a different way of reporting than I had done before.

I took a query writing class from Diane Benson Harrington at Freelance Success. Diane said to mine your life because that's a place to find new ideas. Everybody's seeing the same studies and press releases, but if you have something interesting going on with your life, that gives you an entrée.

However, it's important not to just say, "I had this experience so that makes it important enough to make a story." I found other people who had the same experience I did — people who went to the ER and it was a waste of time. I have a quote in there from one of the dads. I think that rounded out the query by telling the editor that it happened not just to me, but also to other people.

I quoted a statistic I found in the February issue of *Pediatric Emergency Care*. Sometimes there's such serendipity — I'll be going through a study or a magazine and say, "Wow, that's perfect for what I'm working on!" Or I'll have an experience in my life and say, "Oh my God, I just saw a study about that a few months ago." But you don't want to just query on the study. You want to extrapolate on the study and get an idea that's more unique and pinpoint it to something that has a more interesting spin. That's the biggest challenge of pitching magazines.

This query was really long. I was really scared about the whole length thing because I had heard so often that you need only two to three paragraphs. Diane said if you can pack as much information as editors like to see in the query, don't worry about the length. It's a lot more work at the beginning, but I notice I get a lot more response with a more fleshed-out query. Also, I think, "Well, if I sell this, half of the reporting will have already been done."

I always include a title in my queries. Editors think in terms of cover blurbs, so think about what you want that cover blurb to be. Editors are very tunnel-visiony; they're busy and crazed and they're looking for something that fits into their mindset of their magazine. Changing the entire editorial strategy to fit your idea is not going to happen.

Also, when you write a title, it helps to focus you as a writer. If you can't sum up what your story is going to be in five to seven words, maybe you need to step back and say, "Is this focused enough?"

When it came to interviewing experts for the query, I was kind of lucky. I worked in Michigan as a health writer, so I have good contacts at the hospitals out there. I know the women at the University of Michigan very well; they know my work and they've been supportive of my idea of freelancing. So I just called my contacts over there and explained what I was looking for.

The Editor: Christine Porretta, Associate Editor of Health and Nutrition

This idea struck me because it was well developed and well researched. Cynthia made it easy for me to assign the story. Usually I write a detailed assignment letter, but I was able to defer to her proposal because it was that good. This was a blind pitch, but I had confidence in assigning it to her because I saw how much thought she'd put into the proposal.

Cynthia had a great lead anecdote with a personal angle. A personal angle isn't necessary, but she had one and it was perfect. If a writer pitched the same topic except the lead anecdote was from another family, that would be fine. I also like that Cynthia included an anecdote from a real parent other than herself.

Cynthia closed the query briefly, in a succinct way that said what her experience is for writing a story like this. She offered her Web site, which I like — I can just click on the link to see clips. If I need to see more, I can ask the writer for additional clips.

The fact that Cynthia pitched a sidebar — and that it was a polished one — impressed me. She even suggested a title. Whether or not we use it doesn't matter, but we might, because it's a great title.

The query was long, but I had no problem with the length. The general rule is to keep it to a page, but I didn't mind the length in this instance because she didn't include any superfluous information. The pitch flowed well, and her story idea was presented in a logical way.

Better Nutrition

Coffee? Old news. Shade grown, fair trade coffee? A trend worthy of a query. Use your natural curiosity and research skills to find fresh new information about a topic that interests you.

This query is also a case study in the necessity of following up. Writer Amy Paturel didn't get the assignment on the first try; she had to follow up with the editor. In fact, she estimates that a large percentage of her assignments come from follow-ups. So don't get bummed when you don't hear back from an editor — shoot her an e-mail or phone call to remind her of the wonderfulness that is your query.

Dear Carey,

I'm a journalist in Los Angeles and a fellow FLXr [member of Freelance Success]. I have a background in health and nutrition and have written for such publications as Health, Self, Cooking Light, Alternative Medicine and Men's Health.

I think the following idea is a great fit for the Better Eating section of Better Nutrition. The distinction of this new study about liver cancer — on 90,000 Japanese subjects — is of particular interest. Add to that, the growing interest in Shade Grown varieties of coffee, and I think this is a timely topic of great interest to Better Nutrition readers.

Coffee: For the Birds?
The bevy of coffee options is overwhelming, what with espressos, lattes, cappuccinos, flavored and standard drip. And with recent evidence that coffee not only improves mood, but also reduces the risk of type 2 diabetes, Parkinson's disease and liver cancer, Java junkies have even more

reason to imbibe. At least six studies show that people who drink coffee on a regular basis are up to 80 percent less likely to develop Parkinson's disease. Another three indicate that coffee drinking significantly reduces the risk of type 2 diabetes (substances in coffee called quinides increase the capacity of the liver to use glucose, theoretically improving blood sugar control). And, a recent study of 90,000 people published in the Journal of the National Cancer Institute found that frequent coffee-drinkers had half the risk of liver cancer of those who never drank coffee. The drawback: next to tobacco, coffee is sprayed with more chemicals than any product consumed by humans.

"Coffee: For the Birds?" will discuss the increasing availability of organic, shade grown and fair trade coffees, offering health and conservation conscious consumers opportunities to enjoy their Java without a side of cancer-causing pesticides. Readers will learn about the differences between 100 percent organic, 100 percent fair trade and shade grown (one of the environmental distinctions is that shade grown varieties provide sanctuary for birds and effective pest control for coffee plants). Currently, sales of organically produced, shade coffee represent 1 percent or $30 million of the U.S. market for coffee beans. We'll compare environmentally friendly varieties to sun grown coffee, including cost, flavor, health benefits and availability, and provide readers with tips for selecting their personal Java.

In the Kitchen will share innovative ways to incorporate coffee into the diet — even for readers who skip the daily cup of joe. A sidebar will highlight delicious coffee recipes such as Cornish Hens with Coffee Liqueur Sauce, Brazilian Coffee Cookies and Ham with Red Eye Gravy.

I will speak with nutrition experts and lead

investigators of many of the studies listed above, to support the information presented.

I'm sure you will be deluged with queries today after yesterday's FLX [Freelance Success] Market Guide, but I wanted to take the opportunity to introduce myself, particularly since I'm also based in Los Angeles!

If you have questions or would like to discuss the piece, please contact me at xxx@xxx.com or by phone at xxx-xxx-xxxx.

Thanks, Carey. I look forward to hearing your thoughts.

Best,
Amy Paturel, M.S., M.P.H.

The Writer: Amy Paturel

I'm friends with a very eco-friendly guy who used to get on my case because I drank regular coffee. He said I should drink shade grown, fair trade coffee. The next thing you know, I was researching it. I was intrigued, and I wanted to understand where my friend was coming from, and it sent me on an Internet journey of Google searches. I even went to coffee shops and picked up pamphlets about it.

Most people have heard about shade grown and organic coffee but don't know what the terms mean. The fact that they're cropping up in Starbucks and mainstream coffee shops shows that people need to know what they mean. It's a trend that most people don't know much about.

My queries usually aren't this long, but I was just so into it...it just came out of me and I didn't want to stop it. It's also a complicated subject, and I wanted to give the editor a full picture of what I planned to cover.

For the recipes sidebar that I suggested, I wouldn't have to come up with recipes on my own. There's an organization called Copia, the American Center for Wine, Food, and the Arts. It's wonderful in terms of providing recipes to participants and the media.

I think following up is 90 percent of this business; I'm relentless with following up. This article wasn't assigned right away — it was a follow-up. Editors are busy, and if you don't remind them of your query it can fall through the cracks. I schedule follow-ups in my Outlook calendar; as a general rule, I follow up after two weeks.

The Editor: Carey Rossi, Editor-in-Chief

What first grabbed my interest in this query was the news peg of the liver cancer study and the timeliness of shade grown coffee interest. These things demonstrated to me that Amy was up on current research and understood what *Better Nutrition* magazine does — help readers be better consumers of health food. Many of the queries I receive don't do this. I usually have to take a writer's idea and provide the packaging. With this query, I didn't have to do that because Amy had already done her homework — found out what I wanted from an FLX [Freelance Success] interview, done her research and thought about how she could take this pretty common article idea of coffee and make it work for a magazine about shopping for natural health.

I think it's great when writers cite a lot of research. It shows me that he/she is willing to do the homework. Going through scientific studies isn't easy, but if you are willing there is a wealth of knowledge and sources to be had. By citing research, Amy showed me that she was willing to find credible and knowledgeable sources that would make this article informative and well-researched. To me, these are some of the most important aspects to a good article.

Not having experts quoted in the pitch is fine by me as long as there is some research cited or they are named. I think I became leery of experts' quotes in queries after a writer used a quote from someone that had appeared elsewhere. I assigned the article based on that quote and expert. Then in the fact-checking of the article, I found out she had lifted the quote and it was wrong. On another note, letting me know who you plan to interview is great; especially when it comes to the alternative health industry since there are so many unreliable sources. This way I can see how discerning you are about the people you choose to interview.

Query Letters that Rock

Amy's query is straight and to the point. More important, it is easy to read. If you lose me in your first or second paragraph, then I am sending you a rejection. I look at this way: If you can't hold my attention in a pitch, then the article won't be any better. With Amy's pitch, I know exactly what I am getting and why it is important to the reader. I don't have to do any extra thinking. Even her suggestions of sidebars helped me. We didn't use them but I appreciated her thinking of them. Usually sidebars are great additions to articles and many of them are thought of in-house. Amy gave us suggestions, and ultimately that makes my job easier because it is one less thing that I have to conceptualize and do.

The fourth paragraph is what sold this article to me. It outlined the article and spoke to educating the consumer about making buying decisions when it comes to coffee. The only thing that I might suggest is that the third paragraph be tightened a bit so the selling paragraph comes a bit sooner. But it wasn't a hindrance so it isn't something that needs to be done.

Know your market. Writing is a business like any other, and should be treated as such. It is a profession that everyone thinks they can do. No one thinks that they can be a surgeon and go into an operating room and perform, but everyone thinks they can write. As a writer, it is important to prove that you're a professional, not just someone writing on a whim. Know the publications you want to write for: their voice, their tone, what they have done before and what their competition is doing. If you understand this business, your pitches will resonate with editors.

Writer's Digest

"Bitch-slap." Not a phrase you'd expect to see in a query, but sometimes a writer needs to take a risk. Writer Jacquelyn Fletcher researched her market and decided that she could take a chance on using the risqué phrase in her very first sentence. In this case, it paid off.

Dear Ms. Godsey:

There are as many ways to "bitch-slap" the inner censor as there are writers. What works for a while, may not a few years down the writing road, and a new strategy will have to be employed to get around the paralyzing voice of the inner critic. Every writer knows that having the critic is a part of the writing life, but it can be career busting for freelance writers who depend on their flow of words to put food on the table.

I propose a how-to article that would provide fun and creative ways freelance writers can use to get around the censor, including:

* Physical rituals. I visualized my censor as the character Gollum in the Lord of the Rings. I went to Target and bought a toy of the evil monster and every time I feel yucky, I push the button so I hear "MY PRECIOUS," in its creepy recorded voice. Then I can laugh at myself and keep writing. Another writer I know thought of her censor as a prissy Barbie doll. She bought a doll and every time she gets stuck with the critic, she drops it into her metal trashcan.

* Acting class. I use a technique I learned in method acting classes when I'm feeling really lousy. I think of someone I admire who I believe is extremely confident. I pick something I can do to remind me of that person. Then I do it when I'm writing. I wear sunglasses inside, straighten my

hair or curl my lip.

* Rejection letter contest. Find a buddy and send out as many query letters as you can. Whoever receives the most rejections wins. I recently won a lovely Coach bag.

* "It's Their Loss" notebook. Keep a three-ring binder filled with all of your rejection letters. Write on them phrases such as, "Too Bad, Suckers!" "You're Loss!" and "I Win!"

The goal of the article is to help writers continue writing, even when they are battling the inner bad guy by turning the avoidance of the critic into a fun-filled game.

I have written hundreds of magazine articles in addition to non-fiction books, brochures, Web content, and a variety of other projects in the name of my motto: Will Write For Food. I am a columnist for Experience Life, a national health and fitness magazine and editor of Minnesota Bride and Minnesota Meetings & Events magazines. My teaching experience includes a class at the Loft Literary Center in Minneapolis called Freelancing: Living the Writer's Life.

Feel free to contact me at xxx@xxx.com or xxx-xxx-xxxx. I look forward to hearing from you.

Sincerely,
Jacquelyn B. Fletcher

The Writer: **Jacquelyn Fletcher**

This idea came about when I was talking with a friend in New York who is also a writer and she said she pictures her censor as a giant beached whale. I thought that was hilarious. I started thinking, "How can I put my inner censors into a physical thing that's symbolically easier to deal with?"

I was afraid that using the phrase "bitch-slap" wouldn't go over well with the editor. I worried about it for a couple of days. Eventually I put it in because it is what it is. I did risk offending someone, I suppose, but I figured the editor was also a writer so she'd understand. From knowing the magazine and reading it, I had a feeling I wasn't going to offend her. I would never do that with, say, *Christianity Today*.

The two biggest things that I tell my students are to make sure you do your homework and to really hook the editors in the first two sentences, which is why I put "bitch-slap" in there. I usually don't read a query past the first two sentences.

Sometimes I include a proposed title with my query and sometimes I don't. As an editor, I like to see a title on the story when it's turned in, but on the query letter I don't care.

I interviewed people for the query letter. It wasn't hard to find them. Some are friends, some are students, and some are writers who write for me. I also interviewed creativity expert Rosanne Bane, author of Dancing in the Dragon's Den, about the saboteur and the creative process. I interview people before because I need to know if there's enough of a story there to pitch it. Then when I write the query I include as many specific details as possible. It's a mini version of the finished article. In fact, entire paragraphs from my query letter ended up in the story that was published.

The Editor: **Kristin Godsey, Editor**

The fact that Jacquelyn used the phrase "bitch-slap" showed me her voice right away. I can see how that would turn a lot of people off. Me, I was amused by it. It's more modern, more the voice we're looking for; we're trying to be more savvy and up-to-date. It was especially good timing: I'd been at the magazine for six months at that point and was trying to infuse it with a new voice. However, we didn't use the phrase in the article itself.

I liked Jacquelyn's voice and the examples she gave made me laugh out loud...they were so unique. I like the way she spelled out the idea so I'd see exactly how the piece would be formatted. It wasn't difficult to look at this pitch and see what I was going to get.

There is one typo, but my feeling is that one typo is not going to kill you. If the query is riddled with errors or a general sense of sloppiness, that's a red flag for me. I don't want to spend a lot of time correcting someone's grammar and punctuation. But if I really like the idea and the voice, a typo or two will not keep me from buying it.

I have heard from writers who have written to apologize for making an error in their queries. I would think you wouldn't want to draw attention to it. I would be surprised if any editor would let a great piece go because of a typo; it seems like shooting yourself in the foot. There is one person, though, who spelled my name wrong and then followed up and copped to it, and I did appreciate that. I think she recognized what a stupid mistake that was.

Jacquelyn mailed her query. E-mail is definitely becoming more common and more acceptable, but I find that a lot of people still don't have good Web sites where their clips are easy to view. I like getting a query via regular mail if it's someone I've never worked with because I can see their clips. But there are a lot of editors who really prefer e-mail.

Jacquelyn's list of credentials was good. The breadth of her experience is helpful to see. The fact that she's been an editor shows me she knows the editorial process and probably won't be difficult to work with.

The way Jacquelyn structured this query was ideal. She outlined how the piece will look, gave a clear view of her style, and sold herself but didn't oversell herself. I don't like it when writers say, "So-and-so said my piece is brilliant," or try to overplay a really small clip, like telling me their op-ed piece was published in the local paper and pushing it as a big deal.

5280: Denver's Mile High Magazine

Not every magazine wants "just the facts, ma'am." As this query shows, magazine editors will salivate — even leap up from the couch in the middle of Sunday afternoon football — over a query that tells an interesting story with a distinct voice.

Moreover, this query is proof there's no law that says you have to have a stack of clips and decades of experience to nab a plum assignment. Just find a good story, write it well, and soon the gods will bless your bank account.

Dear Cara,

I'm hoping you'll consider the attached pitch letter detailing a story I'm working on. We were in touch last fall regarding a piece I was writing at the time, a profile on Boulder Nordic skier Tara Sheahan. That story ended up on the cover of the Middlebury Magazine in February. I've included a link to it below so you can get a feel for my narrative abilities. I've also included links to two additional narrative features, and have attached my résumé in MS Word format. When I originally contacted [another editor at 5280] about the Sheahan story, those were the tools she said you guys need before deciding on a pitch. Thanks in advance for considering this pitch, and please let me know if you need any more info.

Best,
Devon O'Neil

Searching for Snuffy

The elderly man with a white sun-protection strip over his nose walked up to me from behind. "Excuse me," he said, "but would you mind taking

---

our picture?" I didn't want to. I was tired from skiing all morning, and lying in the snow with the sun on my face was everything I needed right then. Certainly anyone else in the crowd at the top of Vail's Blue Sky Basin would've been capable. For some reason, he chose me.

When I obliged, he took out his camera and signaled to his three friends to come over. He extended an old, 35mm film handheld that seemed a decade past its time. I sized up the men as they gathered. They looked far too old to be skiing, yet there they were nonetheless, with modern equipment and, apparently — if they'd gotten this far — mountain know-how. I noticed a small white sticker at the tips of each of their skis. A closer glance revealed the 10th Mountain Division logo and their names printed below it. Immediately I knew: these were World War II veterans, and ski pioneers of an endangered kind.

I snapped a few photos of them as they flashed weathered yet genuine smiles. Then I asked them the same question I've asked every person I come across with ties to the 10th Mountain Division: "Does the name Snuffy O'Neil ring a bell to any of you?" One of the men, who had already begun to walk away, swung his head around like he'd heard a ghost. "Snuffy O'Neil, did you say?" Before I could answer him, the man who'd approached me initially repeated the name. "Snuffy O'Neil." He shook his head and paused for a moment, collecting his thoughts. "Why, I haven't heard that name since before the war ended." My mind raced as I did the math. Sixty-one years. And yet he remembered.

I told them that Snuffy O'Neil was my grandfather. He died six months before my twin brother and I were born. Aside from relatives, I had never met anyone who knew him. They were the first.

This is how my quest began: through a gift of fate. In the days after this encounter at Vail, I followed the weeklong 10th Mountain Division reunion tour to Ski Cooper, where the original troops were trained back in 1943 and 1944; to downtown Leadville, where the men now walk the streets hunchbacked and historic as the enduring brick buildings that surround them; and in Frisco, at a banquet to remember the tie that bonds them all together — a tie that has inspired books, movies, and which has created a legend.

My subsequent research and interviews painted a picture of a man I wish I'd known. Snuffy O'Neil was a standout skier and rock climber, and was chosen to serve in the prestigious Mountain Training Group (MTG), a division of the 10th which trained the mountain troops for battle. He was a marvelous artist, one who penned cartoons and caricatures that made him a well-known name around Camp Hale and later Aspen. Snuffy also gained notoriety for falling 80 feet off a sheer rock cliff at Hale, and emerging unscathed — not even a broken bone. In fact, one of the only photographs my brother and I have of him was taken moments before the fall.

This is a story about discovering a part of oneself with a push from fate, as well as an opportunity to characterize in a rare, firsthand manner, a group of men unlike almost any other alive. I've talked with many 10th veterans since the initial encounter on top of Vail; they are not only fascinating, but also a dying link to skiing's history. Some are in their 90s. Others in their late-80s. All have stories to share, both about one of their own, Snuffy, as well as a time when the West was still wild, and they ruled it.

About myself: I am a Breckenridge resident and the sports editor at the Summit Daily News in

Frisco. I am 26 years old. After growing up in the Virgin Islands, my brother and I moved to the Rockies and took up freeheel skiing. We still don't know what brought us, but it makes more sense now.

The Writer: Devon O'Neil

For this story, I wanted a bigger audience than the newspaper I write for. I wanted to write in a longer narrative form and maybe make a little money. I'd sent my Olympic story [referenced in O'Neil's e-mail to *5280*] as a finished manuscript to *Sports Illustrated* and *Outside* before sending it to *5280* last fall — that was my first experience pitching a story as a freelancer. *SI* did get back to me and let me know their space was too tight. Another writer advised me to pitch *5280* if *SI* or *Outside* didn't come through; they're more local, and had a great reputation as a National Magazine Award finalist in two categories the previous year.

Cara turned down my Olympic story, but she encouraged me to pitch again and that had a lot to do with why I sent them the Snuffy pitch. Being invited is totally different from trying to invite yourself. I knew they did a lot of stories on mountain life, and even though they're a city publication, half the reason people live in Denver is for the mountains. Plus, I'd read some really personal stories in the magazine, so I thought *5280* was a good outlet for me.

Two-thirds of this story is my own story — searching for part of me — and the other third is on characterizing the veterans. These guys are 90 years old, and they've been friends for more than 60 years. There's something so strong about their bond — it comes from their love of the mountains, they all told me — that they can talk about stuff that happened six decades ago like it was yesterday. I was just shocked by that, and thought, Goddamn, that's a cool reason to be lifelong friends. It was an honor to know that my grandfather was involved and man enough to be remembered by them.

I kept my pitch letter to a page. One page would whet their appetites, make editors want more. I had a twofold strategy for setting up my pitch: first, to pick a scene that would grab attention —

if a pitch can't do that, then you have no chance. And second, to represent the whole story so well and efficiently in the opening that the editor would know exactly what she's going to get in the finished article.

I put a horizontal line in my pitch letter to separate the opening story from the summary of where the story would lead. This second part is sort of chapters two, three, and four — it's my best estimation of where the story will go. I had only three lines left for my bio, so I put stuff in there that would add to the story and help it sell. I sent this in on a Saturday, and had a response on Sunday.

The Editor: Cara McDonald, Deputy Editor

This is a classic example of when I'm happy to write back to a writer. In a sea of muck, this letter was a gem. There's a personal earnestness and candor here. It isn't super formal; it feels collegial and heartfelt. You don't always see this kind of passion in a query letter. Some writers are very formal in their correspondence with me, but I really like it when people approach me with a "let's talk" attitude, as Devon does in his e-mail ... it's much harder for me to ignore writers who treat me like a friend.

Devon had queried me before. In his e-mail, he reminds me that I'd liked an earlier pitch, which we didn't assign because of limited space in our Olympic issue, and that I'd encouraged him to pitch again. That was a very smart thing to do. We get inundated with queries, so when I encourage a writer, it means something. It means I'm interested enough to feed you hope.

When I read Devon's story idea, I had a good gut feeling about it. I passed it along to our articles editor, who agreed and said, "Junior can write." I let Devon know we would formally assign this in the summer and run it in one of our winter issues. It'll run as a long department piece — probably 1,600 to 2,000 words.

We love it when someone pitches us a story that sounds like a magazine article versus a newspaper story. We see too much newspaper writing in queries — they are heavily quote-driven to show reporting, but not fully developed into analysis and commentary, or developed in a cinematic sense to "show versus tell." Because we're a magazine, we can take a first-person viewpoint, a very personal story, and tie it into a larger story of our state's history that readers are curious about. Devon's story is the kind of story we love.

Wines & Vines

No clips? No problem! Writer Ren Collins got around the no-clips dilemma by wowing the editor with a query that was so detailed and well-written that he was confident the writer could do the job. Also notice that Ren didn't bring up the fact that she had no clips in the query. In fact, she didn't even include a credentials paragraph — she just let the query stand on its own.

Dear Mr. Franson:

Cultivating the Brand

According to a report released by MKF Research, 2004 estimated New York winery sales totaled $420 million. The wineries of New York State rely heavily on tourism and New York liquor stores for a large portion of this revenue. In "Cultivating the Brand," I'll talk with New York vineyard owners — including Bill Merritt of Merritt Estate Winery, Forestville, NY; and Len and Judy Wiltberger of Keuka Spring Vineyards, Penn Yang, NY — and highlight some unique strategies they've used to leverage tourist visits and partner with liquor stores, increasing their brand recognition and sales.

Here are some of the tips I've gathered from preliminary interviews with NY vineyard owners:

Hitting the Wine Trail

Conducted by a program of the New York Wine & Grape Foundation, New York's wine trails have grown substantially over the years. Using the Cayuga Wine Trail (est. 1984) as a model, today almost a dozen wine trails throughout New York's five main grape growing regions now hold tourism events throughout the year. Keuka Spring Vineyards relies heavily on the Keuka Lake Wine Trail for off-season tourist visits. The winery closes for a couple months every winter, but opens especially for events held on the trail. Keuka Springs also hosts its own events at the winery.

Shopping the Mall

Bill Merritt of Merritt Estate Wineries invested what he calls "some dear dollars" into opening a year-round store in Buffalo malls. Although he says that managing a store in a mall probably isn't for everyone, it paid off in spades for him from a marketing perspective. "We were in one mall for 4 years and another for 5. In retrospect it was an extremely expensive but extremely effective way to introduce the product," he says. "We had been in the Buffalo market for 25 years and people had never heard of us. We got exposure, we got prestige, it increased our image." At the winery, Merritt's sales are 90-100% wine. In the mall stores, they sold roughly 65% wine and 35% gift baskets or some wine-related item. Bill states, "The big thing was that people would walk through the mall and see the brand. Brand recognition, brand exposure...for 5 years."

Customer Service

At Keuka Spring Vineyards, owners Judy and Len Wiltberger maintain a presence in the tasting room. They pride themselves in creating a special, personalized atmosphere for their customers. Judy ensures the staff is trained to gain geographical information about their visitors. "Most of our customer base is within about 100 miles. We train our staff, throughout the season, but particularly in the fall, to ask people and to check out where they're from, and we supply them with retailers in the area that carry our wines... we really push that — go buy our wine here...this store in your city carries our wine." Len makes sure that message is coupled with a highly personal and enjoyable experience at the winery.

Into the Liquor Stores

As far as Bill Merritt is concerned, New York liquor stores are Merritt Estate's bread and butter. "They are the ones that keep us alive the rest of the year." The mall stores exposed the Merritt Estate brand to such a degree, that customers began asking for Merritt wines in their local liquor stores. In turn, the liquor stores started ordering Merritt Wines more frequently and in greater volume. Bill states, "We went from 5 cases a month to 10 cases a month to 20 cases a purchase. Sometimes they'd buy 2 and 3 times a month."

Keuka Spring Vineyards has also found New York liquor stores to be useful partners. Len doesn't encounter resistance getting Keuka wines into the stores — his customers have consistently asked for them. Some liquor stores have included Keuka Spring wines in their full-page ads that feature 10 or so New York wines.

Wine on the Web

Judy Wiltberger composes a periodic newsletter to Keuka Spring customers on her email distribution list. The newsletter highlights winery news and invites customers to signature events that are held at Keuka Springs. The letters are personally written — Judy states that people write her back to let her know she should send her newsletters more often! Keuka Springs is currently considering creating a wine club and special tasting offerings to its clientele, all communicated through their website.

TV and Radio

Bill Merritt has a plan to reinforce Merritt Estate's brand exposure through radio and television spots. He has been creative in the way he has approached the media. "We worked trade with radio stations and TV stations, that they would then take a couple thousand dollars worth of wine in trade as well as getting cash, and they then turned around and gave that away to their customers," he says. "And what was wonderful about it is, first off, you are getting a new customer to try it — that is solid gold...on top of that you are getting a TV station or radio station saying, 'Here, I am giving you this for Christmas,' which means they think it's worth giving away. It's worked pretty well for us. We're very excited about our increase in sales."

Merritt Estate currently runs 160 10-second spots on network TV in their local market and reinforces that brand campaign with some local radio spots. Bill is excited about this campaign and already recognizes the impact. "We have people come to us and say, 'Hey, I saw your ad on TV last night.'"

"Cultivating the Brand" will provide your readers with innovative ideas that some New York wineries have created to increase word-of-mouth, brand recognition and overall sales.

Sincerely,
Ren Collins

The Writer: Ren Collins

The editor basically gave me the idea for this query. I had read in one of the market guides that the magazine needed some regional features. I sent an introduction e-mail to the editor saying I'm in New York, and he said he'd love to have regional features from New York, and that they're looking for ideas about marketing and promotion.

In my intro letter, I said that I noticed that *Wines & Vines* was looking for regular features. As a native of California, I grew up going to Napa Valley on the weekends and even took clients there at my previous job. I also mentioned that I'm a former business consultant with experience writing about everything from CRM to supply chain management.

For the query, I Googled for information about New York State wines and came up the New York Wine and Grape Foundation. They have a great Web site that lists all the wineries in New York and has a huge information portal with statistics, economic reports, and so on.

As a new writer, it's hard to find sources to talk to through PR agencies. They want to know right away what publication you're writing for and assess whether it's worth their time to talk to you, so there's a wall there. I went directly to the people who run the New York wineries and found them to be so amazing. They take their time to engage their customers in conversation and educate them about wine. Not everyone got back to me, but the ones who did were very forthcoming and helpful. It was a great experience for me as a new writer.

I went into a lot of detail for the query. This editor didn't know me from Adam and I didn't have any clips to show him, so I wanted to prove two things: That I could come up with credible sources, and that I could write a logical outline for an article. If I wrote a shorter query with fewer sources and said I could get X, Y, and Z and couldn't back it up, the editor might say, "Hm, maybe not," or he might ask for clips.

As for my lack of clips, it was "don't ask, don't tell." I used the query format and my deep research knowledge to give the editor some reassurance that I could do the job. I didn't want to highlight the fact that I hadn't written for a wine trade publication.

My advice to other new writers is to get over the fear of contacting an editor. The more research you do, the more you've really researched your topic and have stats and sources to back it up, the more confidence you should have that you can write a good, structured article. Information is always a great antidote to fear.

Query Letters that Rock

The Editor: Paul Franson, Regional Editor

Ren's query was very complete ... she had come up with some facts that jumped right out at you. Things like that show that the writer has done some research. Trades are different from consumer publications because the people who read them are pretty knowledgeable about the subject and are looking for specifics and credibility. Ren provided this in her query.

You could have written a whole article from her query. It turns out that some of the ideas she mentioned I didn't think would fit in the piece, but I encouraged her to pursue them as separate articles.

The fact that Ren included quotes is unusual — I almost never get quotes in query letters — but it shows that she knows what she's doing and that she's likely to produce the article on time. It was longer than it needed to be — she could have stopped after a couple of paragraphs — but it didn't hurt. Giving too much information is never bad.

Most of the queries I get from writers I don't already work with are pretty far off base. They don't look at the magazine, and they keep wanting to write articles about wine tasting and soft, puffy profiles. We want to know hard facts about what the wineries do, which is what Ren provided in her query.

Having no clips is a problem because we want someone who can demonstrate that they can write. But if someone has an idea relating to something we're looking for, I'll often give them a chance. Ren seemed like she knew what she was doing, and that matters more than whether you have published clips.

E Magazine

Article ideas come from the most unexpected places, so keep those eyes open! Writer Jena Ball started out researching an article on a Nepalese god and ended up pitching a story about bats.

Dear Brian,

"Life has a way of dropping bombshells just when you least expect them," says Amanda Lollar, who was enjoying her life as the co-owner of a small furniture store in the town of Mineral Wells, Texas. Amanda's bombshell weighed only 11 grams (about the weight of a pocket pack of tissues) and was no bigger than a business card. "I was on my way to the bank to make a deposit," says Lollar. "It was one of those miserably hot days when you hate to step outside. Then right in front of the bank I looked down and saw a tiny creature lying on its back baking in the sun."

Closer inspection revealed that the creature was a bat. "My first reaction was a shudder of revulsion," admits Lollar. "Like a lot of people I thought bats were pretty creepy. But the poor thing was obviously suffering, so I scooped it up with a piece of newspaper, carried it back to the shop, and put it in a shoebox. I was sure it was going to die. When it didn't, I knew I had to try to help."

Fifteen years and some 7,500 bats later, Lollar has gone from being leery of bats to being totally dedicated to their health and preservation. Not only has she turned her former furniture store into a rehabilitation center and sanctuary for injured bats, but she's founded a non-profit organization for the care and conservation of bats, co-authored a book on bat rehabilitation, done groundbreaking research on the sounds bats use to communicate, given countless educational tours and talks, and trained more than 150 would be bat rehabbers from around the world.

Perhaps the most surprising thing about Lollar's story is that she is not alone. In Northern California, for example, 64-year-old Pat Winters has been quietly going about the business of rehabbing bats and educating the general public for more than 30 years. Winters is the founder of the California based, non-profit organization known as the California Bat Conservation Fund, which sponsors twelve rehabbers, gives educational talks to local schools, and gives medical aid to injured bats with the goal of returning them to the wild. "My first encounter with bats was at a swap meet," says Winters. "I saw two little brown bats (Myotis lucifugus) in a glass jar for sale. They had no shade and looked pathetic so I bought them for $2.00 and brought them home." One died immediately, but the other lived just long enough for Winters to become enthralled.

In Austin, Texas Barbara French was bitten by the bat bug back in 1984 and now works as Bat Conservation International's (BCI) Conservation Information Specialist, and provides rehabilitative care for 150 to 200 indigenous bats each year as a volunteer for the Wildlife Rescue Organization. She is currently doing research on the mating songs of Mexican free-tail bats.

In the Florida Everglades, biologist Denise Tomlinson is a member of the American Zoo and Aquarium Association (AZA) Taxon Advisory Group for bats, is the co-chair of the Florida Bat Working Group, and directs the Bat World Everglades program. She has had a special fondness for Old World fruit bats ever since "Grace," a Rodrigues fruit bat, one of the most endangered bats in the world, captured her heart in 1985.

The list goes on, and includes some 500 licensed men and women working across the United States and Canada. Though they come from widely different backgrounds and lifestyles, they are united in their commitment to the preservation of bats. "Most people don't realize how intelligent and valuable bats are," says Lollar. But according to Melinda Alvarado, a bat rehabber working out of San Luis Obispo, California, all you have to do is meet a bat up close to be hooked. "They look right at you with their bright little eyes," she says, "and you can see the intelligence and curiosity shining there."

In this piece, "For Love of Bats," I'll tell "E" readers about the growing grassroots campaign to save one of the world's most misunderstood and maligned creatures as seen through the eyes of several of America's most well-respected bat rehabilitators. To help readers understand the importance of bats in preserving ecosystems I'll talk to wildlife biologists who study bats and their habitats such as Drew Stokes of the USGS, Rick Sherwin of the University of New Mexico, and Bill and Dixie Pierson. Finally, I'll debunk the most prevalent and destructive myths about bats by introducing your readers to some of the bat world's most enchanting and memorable characters. Sidebars featuring information about some of the more unique bats of the world can be provided along with excellent photos by the award-winning nature photographer Scott Altenbach.

I am a freelance writer working out of Los Angeles with more than twenty years experience writing for a variety of industries and publications including Mother Earth News, House Beautiful, Backpacker, and the Japan Times. I am the author of the syndicated column, "Halfway Over the Hill" and the founder of an online school for journalists (http://www.thenatureofwriting.com).

Thanks for considering my proposal. I look forward to hearing from you.

All the Best,
Jena Ball

Query Letters that Rock

The Writer: **Jena Ball**

This idea started when I went to Nepal to do an assignment about a Nepali god. In Katmandu, the trees are filled with bats. I'd never seen a bat and didn't know what I was seeing. They were orange with black wings, and they're huge. Then, when I was shopping in the marketplace there, I thought this guy was trying to sell me silver — but he had a bat hanging inside his coat. Its body was about a foot long and it looked so sick. It was looking right at me. I could see that this was an intelligent animal, not a spooky, scary Halloween thing. So when I came back I started doing research.

There's a gal here in Northern California who has been rehabbing bats for over 20 years. I went to see her and got to meet her bats. Once you meet a bat you will never be the same — they're so shy and so gentle. Certain species even purr. How anybody can be scared of one is beyond me.

To find sources to interview, I contacted Bat Conservation International, which has revolutionized people's perception of bats. They have a networking newsletter. Amanda, the source in my lede, knew the woman who is in Northern California. The bat community is really small.

I subscribe to *E* and I know that they like a lot of facts and details. That's pretty much my style. I try to move quickly and include a fair amount of description. The query was so detailed that I hardly had to write anything for the assignment itself. I offered a sidebar because this kind of publication likes tips.

This query was definitely overkill for the FOB he assigned, but I was pitching a feature.

The Editor: **Brian Howard, Managing Editor**

Jena's opening anecdote really grabbed me. It was really well written and it was engaging. I imagined it being a really good lede for an article. I also thought it was funny because a lot of people think bats are creepy.

The quotes were good because they showed that she's serious and has good reporting and researching skills. We get a lot of queries that are just people's personal thoughts on something. We also sometimes get people with an academic background who have good research skills but aren't experienced in talking with people. I can understand that in other publications you can report from research journals, but our format is to have live quotes.

This was a little longer than the average query, but it's organized well. I would say it's probably about half the length of the total piece.

Including a sidebar idea was a good move because it showed how serious Jena was and that she had a good command of the subject. We didn't end up running the sidebar, though, because in the section of the magazine where we ended up running the article we never run sidebars.

The fact that Jena offered photos made us want to go with the idea a little bit more. It seemed like she was very professional and could make our jobs easier. We did use some of the photos.

Using new-to-us writers is somewhat a risk. We've had the whole spectrum of experiences with new writers, from great to pretty bad. We try to be careful. Because we're independent, we don't pay as much as the big magazines, so we end up working with more new writers and writers who are starting out. We tend to take more chances with them then.

Jena's query had a good combination of color, direct reporting, and facts, and also a kind of a unique take. We see a lot of queries with angles we've recently covered, and this is something we hadn't done.

Fitness

Research, research, research! Because this writer specializes in nutrition, she's on top of every study, listserv, and press release on the topic. This helps her snag ideas before other writers get wind of them.

Knowing that real-people anecdotes grab editors' and readers' attention, writer Karen Ansel was creative when it came to finding an anecdote to base her idea on. When you need a real-person source, ask your network of friends and family, contact PR firms that deal with the topic of your proposed article, and post a request for sources on Internet discussion boards that you frequent.

Dear Leah:

Jane Smith [not her real name] — a runner since the age of fourteen — knew all about the importance of hydration when hitting the track. And the 2004 Boston Marathon was no exception. The 27-year-old marathon runner was fastidious about drinking up, especially given the oppressive 86-degree heat. "I drank a lot in preparation for the race, and even asked a few friends how to know if I was drinking too much water," recalls Smith. "I heard that it was really hard to drink enough to be in danger, so I drank whenever I was thirsty — pretty much every mile."

Although Smith started out strong, she started to feel dazed toward the end of the race, swerving as she ran. By mile 20 the medical bikers became concerned and began to follow her. Anxious to complete the race on her own, Smith convinced them to let her finish without supervision. But once she crossed the finish line, her condition deteriorated rapidly. "I really couldn't see and my head started hurting," says Smith. "I was nauseous and I threw up all over the carpet of the

Park Street Hotel. My head hurt intensely and my vision still didn't improve."

Smith was rushed by ambulance to Brigham and Women's hospital where she was admitted to the neurology ward for hyponatremia — abnormally low levels of blood sodium. The cause? A potentially deadly combination of downing too many fluids along with heavy salt losses from prolonged sweating, substantially diluting the sodium in her bloodstream.

While Smith's story is alarming, it could have been considerably worse resulting in seizure, coma and even death. Though it may sound like a rare condition, hyponatremia is actually more common than you might suspect. An April 2005 Harvard University study of 488 runners from the 2002 Boston Marathon found that a whopping 13 percent developed this condition. What's more, women appear to be at even higher risk than men, with 22 percent of all females in the Harvard study diagnosed with abnormally low levels of blood sodium.

My article, "Too Much of a Good Thing?," will zero in on how overhydration can lead to hyponatremia in physically active women. The story will be structured as a first-person account of Smith's experience during the 2004 Boston Marathon and will weave in information your readers need to know about this condition, specifically what it is, how it arises and — most importantly — how to prevent it.

Because hyponatremia often shares many of the same symptoms as heat stroke, a box entitled, "Two Commonly Confused Conditions," will help your readers distinguish these illnesses by outlining the differences between them.

For an expert perspective, I'll speak with leading authorities on hyponatremia such as Christopher Almond, M.D., a clinical fellow in pediatrics at Children's Hospital Boston and lead

researcher of the Harvard University study;
Sandra Fowkes Godek, Ph.D., A.T.C., an associate
professor of sports medicine at West Chester
University in West Chester, Pennsylvania; and
Lisa Dorfman, M.S., R.D., a sports nutritionist
with the University of Miami Department of
Athletics who has herself experienced hypona-
tremia.

Attached is a recent picture of Jane Smith. I'd
love the opportunity to tell her story!

Sincerely,
Karen Ansel

The Writer: Karen Ansel

I work out a fair amount and we dietitians push hydration on people so much. I've heard about terrible situations where people have had too much to drink, especially women. I thought it would be interesting to show this flip side of the coin. I had seen a few studies about hyponatremia and thought *Fitness* would be a match.

I searched high and low for a woman who had experienced hyponatremia and found this woman by contacting the Boston Marathon PR office. I found other women, but they didn't fit the profile — they were too athletic, or not in the age range of the magazine. Finally, on my fourth try, I found someone who seemed to be a good match, and I wrote up the query.

The idea is pretty scientifically oriented and I tried to put in a fair amount of research to back it up. I was trying to get that mix of research along with the woman's story — enough to grab the editor.

Because I write about health and nutrition, I'm on top of every nutrition study that comes out. I scour everything. If it comes out, I find out about it one way or another. There are multiple things I look at: Some journals have a table of contents they'll mail you. Then there are listservs of dietitians, Reuters, the AP.

One of my sources, Christopher Almond, was the lead researcher of a very important study that came out last year.

Another source was one of the writers on Freelance Success [www.freelancesuccess.com]. Her sister was an expert on the topic. The third source was a dietician whom I wanted to use as the main source, but she's a triathlete. I've worked with her before.

The Editor: Leah McLaughlin, Nutrition Director

I think the most important thing that spurred me to assign this idea was that Karen had really thought about the piece from several angles. I often receive queries that are extremely myopic in their point of view, and I'm constantly saying, "Good point, but it's a little narrow," or "But what about ... ?" But Karen seemed to have "edited" her own query by using a critical eye and asking what's missing. She also looked at the piece from an editor's point of view, providing sidebar ideas right off the bat, knowing that that's what our magazine does.

This is a pretty long query. People shouldn't put so much in a query that it scares me off, but I need to see enough to know that there's a full feature there. I think it's one of those "you know it when you see it" things. Some stories are more complicated than others.

The query gave me a good sense of Karen's writing. I need to know that she'll be able to write a 2,000-word article, not just that she can write a good marketing pitch that will get me to hire her. So I like the fact that she wrote it in the way it might appear in the magazine ... she gave me a taste.

It is a plus to include experts; it helps me see that the writer is on top of things. If the experts are from 1972, then most likely her research will be, too. But if they're right now, then I know they'll give the article some freshness.

Karen included a proposed title. This is just a another way for a writer to convey that he or she is thinking editorially. If the writer can't sum up the point of an article in a headline, what makes him or her think I can?

Finally, Karen sent a photo of the woman she was writing about. If the article is to be about a real person, this helps. It's important that the women we feature in the magazine approximate our demographic.

Entrepreneur

As a writer, you deal in information. If you're a good writer, you can take any information you find and turn it into a new topic to pitch to magazines. For example, take this query by Dalia Fahmy; Dalia used information that was cut from an article she wrote to create a whole new query for a different magazine. After all, why waste all that research?

Not only that, but she didn't give up — even when the story was assigned and then killed by two different magazines. As she says, "If you have a well-researched query, it will sell."

Dear Karen,

Peter Capolino says he's fighting a hopeless war. The CEO of Mitchell & Ness, a small Philadelphia-based maker of licensed NFL, MLB and NBA sports jerseys, says counterfeiters are selling more of his goods than he is. Last year alone, he shut down 135,000 eBay auctions offering fake Mitchell & Ness gear.

"It's a very frustrating exercise, but you have to keep going after the bad guys," he complains. "Otherwise they'll take over your business."

Once mainly a blight on large companies such as Nike and Levis, counterfeiting has started taking its toll on small and medium-sized businesses.

In the past decade, the value of counterfeit goods has tripled to about $600 billion, says the US Chamber of Commerce, with US businesses losing $250 billion each year to counterfeiters. Ever-improving technology and the growing popularity of internet shopping have made it easier than ever for counterfeiters to make and distribute goods.

And as small businesses increasingly outsource production overseas, they are giving up more of their trade secrets and exposing their brands, designs and other intellectual assets to theft.

"Small businesses have become much more active players in the global market, but because they don't have offices all over the world, they don't have people who can protect their rights everywhere," says David Hirshmann, a US Chamber of Commerce official in charge of intellectual property. "They might not even know they have a problem until their knock-off is being mass-produced."

As a result, anti-counterfeiting services have mushroomed and more small businesses are turning to them for help.

Two years ago, when he realized that a sole employee checking the internet for fake goods could no longer keep up with a ballooning black market, Capolino hired GenuOne.

A five-year old Boston-based security company, GenuOne scours the internet for unauthorized vendors or obviously fake merchandise, and also makes dyes and chips that can be added to goods during manufacturing so they can later be authenticated.

GenuOne CEO Jeffrey Unger says small businesses once showed little interest in his product but now account for about 30% of revenue.

I would like to write a story that portrays the battle of small businesses against the black market. In this story, I will profile one or two entrepreneurs who are suffering at the hands of counterfeiters, and discuss the ways in which they are fighting back. I will present their stories within the wider context of the intellectual property struggle currently underway between the US and Asian governments.

A New York-based freelancer, I cover everything from interior design to corporate mergers. My stories have appeared in the Financial Times, The Miami Herald, New York Post, National

Geographic Traveler, Institutional Investor and Inc. Magazine.

Before becoming a freelancer, I was a senior segment producer on CNBC's "Squawk Box."

Please let me know if you'd like to see more information or clips; or visit www.daliafahmy.com.

Thanks for your time, and I look forward to hearing from you.

Best regards,
Dalia Fahmy

The Writer: **Dalia Fahmy**

In November 2005, I pitched an idea to *Inc.* magazine about how to make money off intellectual property. The editor asked for more and more information about protecting your brand, but ended up cutting much of it out of the piece. The article ended up becoming more of a study about the maker of marshmallow Peeps — how they were increasing the recognition of their brand and shapes and colors. So I used the information on protecting intellectual property to create a query of five hundred words to pitch to *The New York Times*.

The article was assigned within 24 hours. I started work the next day feeling proud and happy, and I must have interviewed five or six people that day because I was so excited. But some of the people I interviewed told me that another *New York Times* writer was working on the same topic. I contacted my editor, and found out that that was the case, and my article was killed.

Then I sent the idea to *Fortune Small Business*. The editor loved the query and assigned it to me over the phone ... but when he found out that I write regularly for *Inc.*, he called back and said he couldn't assign me the piece.

I tried a couple more small business magazines including *Entrepreneur*. When I followed up a week or two later, the editor said she'd like to assign me the article. One thing this query has taught me is that if you have a well-researched query, it will sell.

I learned a lot about intellectual property while working on the *Inc.* story, and I'm milking that now. I'm not an expert, but it's one more field I feel I can write about knowledgably. Now I'm keeping my eye out for other ideas in that field.

The Editor: Karen Axelton, Executive Editor

I liked that this query started off like an actual article. It catches my attention — if I read this lede in a magazine, I'd keep reading. Many writers start off talking about themselves, instead of starting with the story.

Right away Dalia gets to the point that she's writing about small and midsized business, which shows that she knows who our readers are. Her statistics show that she knows how to do research. She says she'll talk to some entrepreneurs, which is something we would require in an article. I like the fact that she included a lot of different specific sources; sometimes people present vague ideas and they don't know exactly what they're going to write. Basically, Dalia supplies everything we'll ask her to put into an article — experts, entrepreneurs, statistics and quotes — and does it all in an engaging way.

The style of the writing is perfect for us. Dalia packs in a lot of information, has real entrepreneurs and experts, and includes quotes so it's very lively. She writes with a good sense of authority; I can tell she's an experienced freelancer.

The biggest mistake that writers make is to send very vague, general queries. These tend to be from people who aren't experienced freelancers. They'll say things like, "I'd like to write about how to start a business." For us, you have to focus on one angle, such as how to raise money — and even then you have to show us how you'll approach it to make it more exciting, like "Five ways to get money from your friends and family."

Sometimes people who have regional publication experience pitch ideas that are too small. They'll send a query about the charming bookstore in their neighborhood and want to do a 1,400-word feature on that. We wouldn't make that a feature unless there's a way to incorporate it into a story on a national trend. There has to be a wider issue that's relevant to small businesses across the U.S.

Smithsonian

Here we have a writer — Paul Raffaele — who has done some very impressive writing for some very impressive magazines. But both he and his editor at *Smithsonian* stress that one of the things that makes him valuable as a writer is that he's always pitching new ideas. That's right — even the most successful and experienced freelancers don't think they're above querying, and editors love writers who bring them new ideas. So if your goal is to get to the point where editors come to you with ideas, stop it. Stop it right now. Keep generating ideas, and keep pitching — and if you're feeling stuck, use this awesome query to get inspired.

Dear Carey,

I'm merrily going on my way, writing the Peking story, sticking my nose into the boudoirs and the war chambers of this Emperor and that Emperor. It will be ready next week.

In the meantime, I wonder if I could pitch you some time-dependent story ideas I've been working on over the past week for your return. The Afghanistan story was on the list of stories you showed interest in when I pitched that collection of ideas in December. I've been waiting for the opium harvest as the best time to do the story.

Should you choose one, I'd plan to leave at the end of the month and need to do some planning beforehand. I hope you don't think I'm greedy. Three months will have past since I left for the cannibals. It's terrifying how fast time goes when you're enjoying yourself. In the tradition of Kafka, I should go work on some newspaper that publishes only shipping lists, so that the remainder of my career will seem ten times as long.

Best regards, Paul

THE WORLD'S MOST EXCITING POLO MATCH
(Taking place July 7-9)

This is an adventure story of the highest order, weaving in, briefly, the fascinating history of polo with a suspenseful and enthralling tale of the rough and tumble annual battle between two traditional rivals, tough mountain men and ponies on the roof of the world. The story would be told in such a way that the reader really cares who will win and sees it through to the nail-biting climax. It also takes readers to some of the most remote people on earth living much as their ancestors have for more than two thousand years. There is potential for many stunning pictures

The roar of ten thousand spectators mingled with the thud and screech of tribal bands greets the arrival of the polo teams from Chitral and Gilgit in Pakistan's fabled Northwest Frontier Province as they race out onto the flat grassy field in the Shandur pass, 12,000 feet above sea level, a place locals call 'halfway to heaven.' Normally pasture land for yaks, the setting is as spectacular as the game itself with the pass dominated by giant Hindukush snow mountains, 40 of them soaring over 20,000 feet and with the biggest, Trichmir, at more than 24,000 feet.

Nestled amid some of the most spectacular mountain scenery in the world, the pass is an historic place, one of the landmarks of, 'The Great Game,' where British and Russian spies in the 19th century played a risky game of realpolitik with the region's kings and rajahs. Alexander the Great's troops passed through here on their long journey of conquest, and many stayed to marry mountain girls and settle. Today, it is a volatile land with Afghanistan crowding it on the north, west and eastern borders and China overhead.

Polo in the West is a sport of the very rich, but

in these remote valleys it is the national sport of a pony-loving people with each tiny village and town fielding their own teams which play the year round. Tillers of the field, carpenters, schoolteachers, yak herders take to the field with nobles, the aristocracy of polo determined by who is the best player.

The teams play polo closest to its original form. The tough, highly skilled mountain men and their rugged ponies play much the same way as they have for over eight hundred years, the game introduced here by Ali Sher Khan, a descendant of Ghenghis Khan. Unlike modern polo, there are hardly any rules, no referee and the six-men teams go at each other with a wild passion that often results in injury and sometimes death. They use their sticks not only to hit the ball but also to belt the arms and shoulders of their opponents. If a player breaks an arm or leg during a match, he has it quickly strapped and returns to the game.

No one plays this ancient and exciting sport better than the teams of Chitral and Gilgit, the region's two major towns, rivals for centuries separated by 120 miles of narrow high mountain pathway with the Shandur Pass at the mid-point. The annual match is so eagerly anticipated that more than 10,000 spectators flock to the pass from the two towns and mud-hut villages in nearby and distant mountains and valleys.

Most people here still live and dress much as their ancestors have since biblical times. Settled on the slopes and rocky outcrops at the pass, a natural grandstand, the Chitral supporters are kept on one side of the field, Gilgit fans the other with a medieval-like bazaar in between. Because of their fervour for the annual match, several hundred riot police are on hand to prevent any fighting between rival supporters.

Polo began in Persia in the 6th century B.C.,

and as it spread across Central Asia the war-like tribesmen took to it with a passion, using it as a training game for cavalry units. With as many as 100 players on each side, it was like a miniature battle. That zest for the game has never subsided.

Getting to the match is risky enough for the players and their ponies. To reach the field at the Shandur Pass they must make a five-day journey along narrow crumbling pathways that snake across the high mountains with drops of a thousand or more feet.

Ideally, I'd hire a pony and ride along the mountain pathways to the pass with the polo players from one of the teams. Each player is allowed just the one pony for the match, and to acclimatise them as they climb higher each night they play practice games when camp has been made along the trail.

We would meet the major players and follow them through the thrilling final match, between the best players of Chitral and Gilgit. It ends with a victory dance by the thousands of supporters of the winning team who are borne off the field on eager shoulders, heroes through the valleys for the next twelve months.

My friend, Prince Siraj Ulmulk, a grandson scion of Chitral's last king, will ensure that I have the best possible access. I'd also be able to stay at his home, a former palace, to get an idea of how the high and mighty lived in this high and mighty place.

There's more to the story. On the Gilgit side, a couple of hours up the mountain is the legendary kingdom of Hunza where people are said to commonly live to 100 or more. The present king still lives there, and I could bring in the angle of some of the world's hardiest people living in this area, which reflects the tough nature of their favourite sport, polo. They have a Wizard Of Hunza, the latest in a line of powerful shamans who stretch back beyond when Alexander the Great's troops came here. He performs a prophetic ritual, going into a trance and communing with the queen of the snow fairies who gives him a prophecy. The Hunza king claims they usually come true.

On the Chitral side, the area was dominated by the Taliban during their rule across the border, the rugged mountains of Afghanistan being just a few miles away, and the influence of Islamic fundamentalism in the town is still strong. As well, in the mountains perched above Chitral are the Kalash, the original tribe on which the Kipling story and movie starring Sean Connery and Michael Caine, The Man Who Would Be King, are based. They are a colourful people, a small band of pagans living within a sea of Muslims, and are fiercely independent.

Of course, these are side plots giving give the story more colour, but at centre of the story is the mad, wild, fierce polo match on the roof of the world.

[The e-mail contained two more fleshed-out story ideas.]

The Writer: **Paul Raffaele**

I never went to journalism school, instead being trained as a broadcast journalist by the Australian Broadcasting Commission. After eleven years, mostly as a senior reporter and foreign correspondent, I left the ABC to pursue a career in feature writing because I preferred that to broadcast reporting. I plunged in at the deep end, but was lucky because the then editor-in-chief of *Parade* magazine, Jess Gorkin, gave me a number of assignments.

I spent the 90's as a staff writer with *Reader's Digest,* covering the world from my Sydney base. I did animal stories, and have covered the great white shark, Siberian tigers, bonobo apes, African wild dogs, cheetahs, hippos, mountain and lowland gorillas, and Tasmanian devils, among others. I also wrote investigative reports.

Query Letters that Rock

Bishop Belo of East Timor stated that my exclusive article highlighting his brave battle against the Indonesian invaders of his homeland for *RD*'s one hundred million readers worldwide when he was a little-known cleric, helped him win the Nobel Peace Prize in 1996.

My first story for *Smithsonian* was about the African bush meat crisis, and an American helping to save the gorillas in Central Africa. I pitched it first to Carey Winfrey, editor-in-chief of *Smithsonian*, and he assigned it. I've worked for many superb editors with major magazines worldwide, but Carey turned out to be by far the best. I so enjoyed working with him on the bushmeat story that ever since I've given him first choice of my story ideas.

I've been writing similar articles, though with much less words than for *Smithsonian*, for three decades. I like to go to remote places for my stories. I'm not sure what a traditional query to an editor is, I just put down the elements of what I feel will make a compelling story for the readers.

I don't normally send more than one pitch to an editor at a time. I like to focus on one story idea. However, the stories in this pitch were all occurring in early to mid July.

I learned about the polo match between these traditional rivals when I was in Chitral and Gilgit in Pakistan several years ago on a story for *Reader's Digest*. I'd been to the Shandur Pass, 12,500 feet above sea level, where it takes place.

My main method for researching my queries is to read as many newspapers and magazines as I can lay my hands on every day, always looking for story ideas. I also watch a lot of documentaries, especially on National Geographic and Discovery channels, looking for story ideas. When I find a story that I like, and I only pitch stories that I want to do very much, then I'll go on the Internet and to libraries looking for material to support my pitch. For the polo match idea, I went onto the Internet searching for material, went to the state library in Sydney for more research, and e-mailed friends I have in the region.

I don't wait for assignments to fall into my lap. Every day of my life I am looking for new story ideas and, as the saying goes, I am only as good as my last story. I have never been given an assignment by an editor that I didn't pitch because I am always knocking on the door, offering new story ideas. I think editors like this approach.

In the pitch I mention Prince Siraj Ulmulk. I met Siraj while I was in Chitral for the *RD* story. I don't think my friendship with Siraj made a difference in the pitch, as such, though it will help me in my reporting of the story. The only tip I can give for other writers is to enjoy making friends such as Siraj on the road.

If you want to do the kind of writing I do, if you're married or in a relationship, you need to have an understanding family because you might be spending much of the year out on the road. It can be lonely, but that's the balance against the pleasure of doing these kinds of stories. You also get to spend 24 hours a day with your family when you're home.

Don't be disheartened if an editor knocks back your pitch. Sometimes, I have to offer several story ideas before one is accepted. If a writer has talent, courage, patience and the ability to sleep sitting in the open in the jungle all night with monsoonal rain pouring onto you, and eat spiders and locusts, and not panic when a clan of naked cannibals brandishing bows and arrows ambushes you on a remote river (as happened on my most recent assignment, in Indonesian New Guinea), then he or she will have no trouble becoming part of my tribe, the nomadic freelance feature writer.

The Editor: Carey Winfrey, Editor-In-Chief

Paul has written for us for a couple of years now and has an absolutely spectacular sense of the magazine and where the magazine's needs dovetail with his interests. He lives in Sydney, Australia, but a few months ago he visited us here in Washington and brought along about 25 story ideas, which we went over verbally. Of the 25, there were 20 that were great! He's someone who really understands the magazine.

It's amazing how many queries we get from people who are obviously sending out the same one to the *Atlantic Monthly, Sports Illustrated, Cooking Light,* and on and on. A query like that inevitably belies a total misunderstanding of the magazine.

Even though he's written for us many times, Paul conveys the enthusiasm of a 19-year-old. He doesn't think, "I'm a big star, therefore whatever I want to do I can do." He knows he's got to sell the idea, and his enthusiasm is contagious. Some writers who have a relationship with a magazine wait for the editors to assign stories to them, and that's fine — but if you're trying to get your work in as many publications as possible, you do have to pitch. You've got to sell the story and tell the editor what it is about the story that will work for the magazine.

We get about 4,000 queries a year. Because of that volume, an editor's reflexive response to queries here is "no." After all, if you respond affirmatively you have to talk to the writer, help shape the idea, negotiate how much to pay, put through documents and on and on. Giving a green light is taking on a burden of obligation. Sure, that's part of your job as an editor, but it's not the fun part and you don't want to do it any more than you have to. After all, you have only so many pages to work with. So you tend to say no to writers who misspell the name of the place they want to visit or don't seem to understand what your magazine is trying to do or, in my case, address me as Ms. Winfrey when I'm a guy. You're looking for a reason to say, "This one is not worth my time."

There are a number of locks, like on the Panama Canal, that the query writer has to go through. The letter has got to be perfect: no grammatical or punctuation errors. The first paragraph should indicate that the writer knows how to put words together. The second shows that the writer understands what the magazine is about. The third shows that the writer has a great idea. In the fourth, the writer explains why it's a great idea for your particular magazine. The fifth paragraph makes the case for why it should be done now. And the sixth explains why he or she is absolutely the best possible person in the Western hemisphere to pull this story off. That's a lot of locks to get through. People who think they can write a couple of paragraphs of boilerplate query are kidding themselves.

Paul pitched three ideas, and I assigned the polo story. Any of his three ideas would have worked; the polo story just seemed to have a lot of interesting elements and didn't conflict with anything we had done or have in the works. With Paul, I'm always looking to say "yes." I want to keep him busy so he doesn't take his ideas to someone else.

It was fine for him to send along more than one idea, but I'm lazy and I don't want to read twelve ideas at once; I've got a magazine to put out. I used to get queries from a good *Smithsonian* writer who would pitch eight or ten ideas at the same time and his letter would sit unread in my inbox because I never had the time or the energy to deal with all the ideas. (He finally gave up, I'm sorry to say.) Two or three ideas is fine if you have a relationship with the magazine. If you don't, find one idea that really works.

On the whole you want to keep your queries short, but if you have a great idea that you're excited about and it takes longer than a page, do it. Rules are made to be broken — if there's a good enough reason to do so. Remember, the query is the one opportunity you get to show what you can do. You're trying to get the editor's attention, just like when you were a teenager and trying to catch the eye of the opposite sex (or maybe the same sex). You want somehow to say, "I've got something here to offer; I'm a bit special," without being a kook or scaring the person off. Be distinctive but not crazy.

Paul doesn't need to include credentials because he's written for us before, but for a new writer, it's critical for the editor to know the writer's experience. Don't list every single magazine you've published in; writing for *The New Yorker* is better than writing for five or six farm journals or trade magazines.

Everything a person does in a query letter is going to be judged as an indication of whether the writer is useful to pursue or not. If you start bragging in a letter, it will turn the editor off, but if you're too modest, the editor will think you can't pull it off. It's a fine line.

Graduating Engineer & Computer Careers

Sometimes a personal referral can work wonders. Not that writer Jebra Turner's query wasn't awesome on its own — it was — but if you drop the name of a writer the editor knows and trusts (with the writer's permission, of course), the editor may be more likely to give your query more than a quick skim. Massaging the editor's ego a bit doesn't hurt, either.

With Jebra's query, you'll also see the value of mining your current or previous occupation for ideas.

Dear Tim,

I've heard good things about you from my colleague X — she mentioned the sorts of topics you may be interested in for Graduating Engineer Magazine. As a freelance journalist for a dozen years, I've written publicity materials and articles that appeared in many publications, including Oregon Business, Fast Company, and the Christian Science Monitor. Previous to that I was human resources manager at a spin-off of the high-tech giant, Tektronix. And while I studied business at Oregon's major urban university, I worked as a peer adviser in the career placement office. There, many of my clients were engineering majors.

Here's an article idea that may be helpful to minority engineering students ready to enter the workforce:

CAN I WALK A MILE IN YOUR SHOES?:
HOW A "SHADOW DAY" ENLIGHTENS
It's a common complaint among employers — freshly minted engineering graduates who don't understand the field — or how they fit in it. How can you avoid bumbling and stumbling during job interviews or the first days at work? Scope out

---

your dream job or workplace in advance. Arrange to follow around for a day an engineer who's already doing what you want to do.

I can give readers a step-by-step guide to getting the most out a shadow day — even tell them how to target and cold-call the ideal "shadow-ee." For example:

—Be strategic. In choosing an engineer to shadow, ask: Who's employed at my top-pick organization? Who's doing work that I want to "road test"? Who's new in the field and still charged up? Who's seasoned, with experience that's wide or deep? Who has contacts they'd be willing to share?

—Make it count. As a "shadow-er" you should observe and, if possible, participate in the actual work. And don't give yourself an easy pass on unpleasant tasks or working conditions, either. If it's typical in that department to work 24/7, don't think you can drop in at 9 and skip out at 5. Not if you want to experience the real deal.

—Emphasize the personal aspect. You'll get the most out of your shadow day by having coffee, lunch, or after-work drinks with your shadow-ee and co-workers. People often let their guard down around food and drink, so you'll get a truer picture of the position and the organizational dynamics.

Does shadowing really prepare graduates to enter the engineering world? Yes. Though occasionally, it has the opposite effect. I once set up a shadow day for an engineering applicant who discovered she was too much of a "people person" for the profession. She became a flight attendant instead. Usually, though, the outcome is a savvier — and happier — engineering job applicant or new-hire.

I look forward to applying my skills to benefit Graduating Engineer Magazine!

Best regards, Jebra Turner

Query Letters that Rock

The Writer: Jebra Turner

I know that it's tough to get in with editors. Even if they do like a query, the reception is most often only lukewarm. This idea sold right off the bat, and I'm sure that although the idea is a good one, it was that personal connection and referral that clinched it. I think having a referral goes a really long way.

How to get those leads, and referrals, and introductions, though, that's the quandary. Especially when you're a novice, or shy, or live out in the sticks. Well, I've met writers through classes (both online and off), association meetings, critique groups, book signings and poetry readings, writers conferences, and friends of friends. I got to know these people better by asking them out for coffee or a meal, and then I kept in touch. Some of them later referred me to their editors, or gave me a heads-up about new magazines in the works, or as editors themselves, assigned articles. Very kind.

I stressed my personal experience because it seemed that that was what I had going for me. I didn't have a lot of experience writing articles, so I went back to see what I had done and what I knew about. Because I worked for a company that had a shadowing program for internal employees, I saw what it did for employees when they got a look at other jobs. Once a warehouse person shadowed a salesperson, they might say, "I couldn't do that job." Or sometimes they did like it and would want to get into some a training program.

I went into a lot of detail to flesh out the idea; it was kind of a weird one, and I didn't know if the editor would understand what it was. I'd written a press release about the shadow process for the company I had worked for, so I had all those bullet points anyway, though I had to recycle them for a college scenario rather than a corporate scenario.

The Editor: Tim Clancy, Publisher, Alloy Education

The introduction was great because Jebra mentioned someone I know, stroked my ego a bit, mentioned some of the publications she's written for, and talked about experience relevant to our marketplace. It's everything I would look for in a potential writer.

The personal connection was clearly the first thing that this query had going for it. I saw the name there and that was a good thing; it appealed to me on a personal level. That was the kicker that got me to really read it carefully as opposed to skimming it.

The topic certainly caught my attention. The title of the article was in all caps, so even if I was going to skim the query it would jump out. Having done this for so many years, I get a lot of queries about how to ace an interview and how to write a resume. Job shadowing is hot and we haven't really covered it in our publication.

I think whether you need to include quotes from sources depends on the article. If Jebra had specifically identified companies or universities that sources were from, it may have grabbed my attention more, but the topic was strong enough to do that on its own. If the idea weren't as strong, I would need some unique angle or for the writer to talk to companies we were related to through advertising. We don't do advertorial, but if a source was someone I knew was either a current or a past advertiser, I could go to my sales rep and say, "Dr. so-and-so from company X is being quoted in an article."

I like the way Jebra did the bullet points. I get some things that are way too detailed and others that are too rudimentary. When I'm busy, it's nice to have something that straddles that line.

Jebra didn't offer published clips. Because of the nature of what we do, it's not as critical; we have quite a few writers for the nursing magazine who are nurses, not writers. If someone hasn't been published before, I will take a gamble from time to time. It's risky because sometimes you get someone who sounds great and then the article comes in and it's a nightmare. But that's what editors are for. On the other hand, there are cases where we've had people who had been published a lot and they send in articles that are terrible.

An editor can often tell from someone's correspondence if she's able to at least put things on paper. It's the writer's experience and angle and in some cases the people she says she can get hold of that influences me to assign the piece.

This query didn't have mistakes and it was well organized. It was informative and piqued my interest without overshowing the idea. It was a good balance.

mental_floss

They say laughter is the best medicine. What they don't say — but they should — is that laughter can land you article assignments. Injecting a little humor into your query shows the editor that you have a personality to go along with your awesome ideas and sharp writing style. And as you'll see here, a bit of joking can help banish what writer Rick Chillot calls "the stink of desperation" from your query.

Ms. Harris,

Hello, I'm an experienced freelancer who's very keen to write for your astonishingly excellent magazine. I can send clips, etc. upon request, but here's a brief treatment of the story I'd like to propose:

THIS GLAND IS YOUR GLAND

Your heart pumps blood. Your stomach digests food. Your brain thinks, except when you're in love. But while these big, media-friendly organs hog all the attention, your glands go unnoticed. And that's a shame, because your glands secretly secrete the solutions to many of life's problems. Without their tireless efforts the rest of your body would function about as well as an automobile with no oil, antifreeze or transmission fluid. Even though you're walking around with a complete set, odds are you have no idea what your glands do. So take a gander at this glandular field guide. Gland ho!

The article will feature brief descriptions of:

■ The Pituitary Gland: The cappo di tutti of hormone-releasing glands.

■ Pineal gland: The body's clock watcher.

■ Thymus: The incredible shrinking gland.

■ Salivary glands: Spitting's not just a nasty

habit, it's a waste of an amazingly versatile liquid.

■ Sweat glands: The good news: your sweat doesn't smell. The bad news: Bacteria that mixes with your sweat sure does.

■ Also: Oil glands, sex glands, thyroid, adrenals, and more.

I hope you'll find that this story idea fits your needs. If not, I'd be happy to pitch some more your way! The mental_floss mission is right up my alley: I've written everything from magazine shorts to feature articles to a complete book, all geared towards converting dry and complex information into comprehensible and lively prose. I'm certain I can do good work for mental_floss; please let me know what I can do for you.

Best,
Rick Chillot

The Writer: **Rick Chillot**

I had been wanting to write something about biology that wasn't service-oriented — how the body works, instead of tips on how to stay healthy. When I saw *mental_floss*, I saw the opportunity to explore that. I had a feeling that glands was a topic they hadn't seen.

A lot of times when I pitch an idea I act as if I've already started writing the article. I went to the library and looked through medical encyclopedias and textbooks; I did enough research to do a little treatment of the topic.

The humorous style of *mental_floss* resonates with my own humorous style. When writing queries, I try not to make it sound like a form letter. As a former editor, I know it's tedious to go through a stack of unsolicited queries. Sometimes I even put a joke at the end of my query, saying, "Even if you're not interested in this idea, here's a joke to entertain you." It's almost like an audition. For example, one of the jokes I've used is, "A guy walks into a psychiatrist's office and says, 'I'm a teepee, I'm a wigwam, I'm a teepee, I'm a wigwam!' The psychiatrist looks at him and says, 'Calm down, you're two tents.' (It makes more sense if you say it aloud.)" In other queries, I've ended with, "Hire me before I do something desperate like write a novel."

I try to write as if I'm in the club and not begging for work. A bit of casualness can help. I think it's a turn-off when a query stinks of desperation.

Editors are lazy, and anything you can do to make their life easier will help your chances. If you can, have a headline so the editor doesn't have to think, "How does this fit into our magazine?" Take the next step.

The Editor: Neely Harris, Editor-in-Chief

The title of this query really grabbed me: "This Gland Is Your Gland." It made me laugh, and one of our goals at *mental_floss* is to educate people in an entertaining and humorous way. My job is to make sure we can make readers laugh, and coming up with good titles is a struggle. Being handed that great title was like — wow. It was as if the writer had done part of my job for me.

I like to tell writers that if you want to pitch a story to an editor, you have to think like an editor. An editor is immediately thinking about what the angle of the story will be, what the hook will be, how it will draw the reader, what section it will go in. The title is part of that.

I laughed at the title, but my next thought was, "How can we possibly make an article about glands interesting?" It sounds like the most boring topic in the world. But then I kept reading and Rick was throwing these really interesting tidbits at me — and he was doing it with what I consider a trademark *mental_floss* style and tone.

When Rick called the article a "glandular field guide," a layout idea immediately popped into my head. I envisioned a map of the human body like the Operation game. Calling the article a field guide was catchy and it had a visual to go along with it. Yet again the writer was doing my work for me.

If you send in an article idea, include where you envision the article being published; have a column or feature spot in mind for your idea.

Try to know the editor's pet peeves. For me, it's this: When people ask me for my editorial calendar and then pick something off the calendar and want to write it, that really annoys me. We have an editorial calendar, but it's very vague and general. I want to hear new ideas from a writer. Based on those new ideas, an editor can get a very clear idea of how well the writer knows the magazine. If a writer looks at an editorial calendar and says, "Oh, I can write about that for you," there's no thought behind it.

Midwest Airlines

What do you do when you get a rejection? If you're like many writers, you spend some time sulking, kicking your desk chair, and pounding down chocolate and wine. But if you're Jeanette Hurt, you turn around and whip another idea right back at the editor while you're still fresh in his mind.

Whenever you get a rejection, the first line in your next query should be something like, "Thanks for your quick response to my query 'Why You Should Hire Me.' Here's another idea for you; I look forward to your reply!" If the editor has invited you to send in more of your fabulous ideas, be sure to remind him of this at the top of your query.

Dear Eric,

Thanks for getting back to me about the Back Streets of Milwaukee tours. Let me know if you find a spot for it in the future, or if you would need me to cover anything else that comes up.

I have another story idea for you that you might be interested in. England's great modern sculptor, Henry Moore, is getting his biggest American show ever — in Grand Rapids, Michigan, at the Frederik Meijer Gardens & Sculpture Park. (If you've never visited it before, it's worth the trip: on par with Rodin's gardens in Paris and Sapporo's sculpture park.) The exhibit runs from January 21 to May 8, 2005, and the sculpture park developed it in conjunction with the Henry Moore Foundation in England.

The show is the only exhibit of its kind in the world. One of the fathers of modernist sculpture, Henry Moore preferred to have his abstract bronzes surrounded by trees than by buildings. In Henry Moore: Imaginary Landscapes, the largest American exhibition of his work, his reclining figures will find a temporary abode among the trees and flowers of the Frederik Meijer Gardens &

Sculpture Park in Grand Rapids, Michigan. The exhibit, which will not travel anywhere else in the world, unveils 85 works, many never seen in the U.S.

I think a short story or a feature about this exhibit might be good for Midwest Airlines Magazine. Please let me know what you think.

Thanks,
Jeanette Hurt

The Writer: Jeannette Hurt

I had another query in the snail mail to Eric when I came up with this idea. The PR person from the convention and visitor's center was doing a fam tour [a familiarization tour] with a press trip. I had never gone on a press trip and had no idea what I was doing. But I went, and one place we visited had this magnificent sculpture garden and museum. I knew from studying *Midwest Airlines* that they did a preview section, and most of them were art exhibits across the country. So when Eric rejected my first query, I had just returned from the press trip and I pitched this idea.

It was an e-mail query, so it was a little less formal than a first blind query where you really try to put everything in the first paragraph. I tried to craft the query to get across the specialness of the exhibit and convey some of the excitement. But if you're too much of a perfectionist, you're never going to get your queries out the door. I got the query out the day he sent me the first rejection.

Stories for the FOB section of *Midwest Airlines* are 300 to 400 words max. You don't want e-mail queries to be these long, involved things, especially when you're targeting such a section. You don't want the editor to have to scroll down to get the gist of the query. They just don't have time.

Query Letters that Rock

The Editor: Eric Lucas, Former Managing Editor

This query is a perfect example of the saying, "Luck is what happens when preparation meets opportunity." Jeannette's query was concise, to the point, and it met a need that I had. The airline said it needed something about Grand Rapids, and lo and behold, there was Jeanette's query about Grand Rapids. It was appropriate for the magazine, accurately aimed at a particular section of the magazine, and told me a couple of things I didn't know about Henry Moore as a sculptor. And she didn't waste my time with anything else.

The best queries are brief and to the point, and convey the idea that they're professionally done with no misspellings or obvious inaccuracies.

This wasn't Jeanette's first query to me. Something I try to explain to writers about queries is that almost never does a specific query meet the specific needs of a magazine editor. Magazines these days have so many precise parameters that you'd have to be a psychic to parse it out on the first try. I tell writers that if you actually sell a story on the basis of a first-time query, you should buy a lottery ticket that day because your karma is really good.

The purpose of a first-time query is to introduce yourself to the editor. If the query is lucid and the credentials are good, most editors will send back the same message I sent to Jeanette: "It's not right, but feel free to send others."

Go ahead and write the query, but you probably will not get an assignment on the basis of that query. Your true goal is to engage the interest of the editor.

It's ultra important to make sure the queries are accurate and grammatically correct. I was receiving ten to twenty queries a week, and I'd have to say that 90 percent of them were unsuitable on the face of it ... they misspelled my name, the idea was completely inappropriate, or they contained an obvious error.

Jeanette's was a perfect query. She did the article for us and it led to three main features. In each case it was me who conceived the idea, but I wanted to hire her.

Oxygen

You have an article that you wrote for a magazine but was killed, or that you wrote on spec but wasn't accepted. Your first impulse may be to send the article to other markets to try to make up for lost time.

Wrong!

Most editors want to see queries instead of full manuscripts so that they can have a hand in what goes into the piece, from the slant to the word count. What are the chances that an article you wrote for a particular market would be just right, as-is, for a completely different magazine? Slim to none. That's why you need to — as writer Beverly Burmeier did — re-query the idea for the new market. Once you've snagged an assignment, you can tweak the original article to fit the new assignment specs.

Dear Lisa Hannam,

Enclosed is a query for a health/nutrition article on snacking — a habit that affects the majority of us, regardless how attentive we are to overall fitness. Understanding motivations for snacking will help us keep it part of a healthy eating plan.

QUERY: SNACK ATTACK — WHAT TRIGGERS YOUR MUNCH BUTTON?
Returning home after a vigorous tennis match, I grabbed a miniature chocolate bar and a handful of peanuts. Anyone who knows me could have predicted I'd grab a snack then; I always reach for comfort food to soothe my competitive juices.

We snack for many reasons — some healthy and some not. My article "Snack Attack — What Triggers Your Munch Button?" will look at four to six different snacking personalities. I'll tell what triggers the need to nibble and explain how each can tweak its snacking options to meet the same needs with better choices. Snacking can be part of a healthy eating plan, according to The

American Dietetic Association — if you choose wisely.

Among the snacking personalities I'll profile for Oxygen readers are these:

Workout Refueler. Normally your body needs to refuel every three to four hours, but if you exercise heavily, nutritional requirements increase. Snacks help the body replace depleted stores of carbohydrate and protein. Instead of a candy bar that's overloaded with fat, dip your spoon into some fruity low-fat yogurt or even the peanut butter jar.

Late Morning Carb Loader. Diets that strictly limit carbs can leave you feeling drained of energy and dehydrated. Snacks high in complex carbohydrates can optimize your energy level and mental power. "Snacking gives me energy and helps me concentrate on my work," says Karen Beuerlein, of Knoxville. Eat oatmeal or wheat toast for breakfast to provide enough carbs to last until noon. But if you need more, try unbuttered popcorn or tortilla chips with salsa for a quick boost.

All Day Nibbler. The munch button for this person is always "on," but there's no need to turn it off as long as the nibbler chooses nutritious snacks and includes caloric counts in the daily total. Research has clearly shown that frequent meals help control hunger and overeating and make it easier for you to consume all the nutrients your body needs. What's more, eating smaller amounts more frequently can reduce the load on your heart and prevent heartburn. Katherine Tallmadge, registered dietician and spokesperson for the American Dietetic Association, says, "I often tell my clients to snack up to three times a day, but limit the calories in each to 100 to 200 calories." Veggie sticks (carrots, celery, zucchini, or sweet peppers) are terrific munchies, especially when eaten with a low-fat dip or cottage cheese.

Tired Eater. When Melissa Baldridge of Denver needs a pick-me-up, she reaches for a cookie and the quick sugar high she gets from sweets. But Tallmadge says that by substituting an apple for a cookie every day, a person could lose up to 20 pounds in a year — with no other change in diet. Keep sweet low-fat snacks like frozen grapes, bananas, or even angel food cake handy to lift mid-day energy plunges.

Doldrums Diner. Boredom from watching too much television or sitting in front of a computer for hours can lead you to crave the crunchies. Stave off chip binging with a healthier snack such as one-half cup pretzels dipped in mustard. Or find an alternate activity: drink hot tea, pet the dog, or take a walk. "For me, working out sometimes substitutes for eating," says Abigail Green of Baltimore.

Other suggested snacking personalities could include the Frenzy Feeder and Nighttime Chocolate Sneak. In addition to Tallmadge, author of Diet Simple, I will interview experts like Nancy DiMarco, Department of Nutrition and Food Sciences at Texas Woman's University, and women like Beuerlein, Baldridge, and Green, who include snacks in their eating plans.

I can include a sidebar of snacks recommended by ADA that provide the right proportions of carbohydrate, protein, and fat — all good options for satisfying a snack attack whenever it occurs.

My writing credits include a variety of national publications such as Ladies' Home Journal, Prevention, Shape, Better Homes and Gardens, Energy for Women, USA Weekend, Christian Science Monitor, Bally Total Fitness, TravelAge West, E/the Environmental Magazine, Woman's World, and others plus dozens of regional magazines and newspapers. I have articles coming soon in American Way, Texas Co-op Power, Live and Learn (an AARP publication), and

ePregnancy.
I look forward to working with you on "Snack Attack — What Triggers Your Munch Button?"

Best regards,
Beverly Burmeier
www.beverlyburmeier.com

The Writer: Beverly Burmeier

I wrote an article on snacking a year ago and got paid for it, but before it got published the magazine folded. The rights were returned to me. I still wanted to see the article in print but felt it needed a different angle. Instead of focusing primarily on the health aspect, I played around with the theme to come up with another salable article.

For the title, I tried to come up with something that was catchy. Snacking by itself will not grab an editor's attention. "Munch Button" had a synergy that appealed to me and a hip twenty-something demographic.

I started the query with a personal anecdote because my experience seemed pretty typical for the readers I was targeting. I also used some quotes from people who were quoted in the original article. All my original sources agreed to help me with this query. The new query contained much of the original research and content — just in a different format.

My queries generally run between a page and a page and a half. This was a new editor I hadn't worked with before; I had to give enough information to tell what I'd cover in the article, but I didn't want to bore her.

I haven't had many situations where I had a complete article that was later turned around and approached as an entirely new piece. It's hard to rethink an idea as a query when you've already written a longer piece. But you don't want to turn in the completed piece, because magazines are generally leery of using an article written for another pub. They want to feel the piece is "new" and was written just for them. Besides, every magazine has a little different slant, even if they are targeted to the same general audience. The query for *Oxygen* was organized and presented in a way that fit its demographic better — and that appealed to *Oxygen's* editor more — even though some of the same research and quotes were used.

The Editor: Lisa Hannam, former Health & Nutrition Editor

The first thing that grabbed me was who Beverly had written for in the past and that they were competitors of *Oxygen*. While a writer may be good in other areas, it's good for me as an editor if she knows our readership and the voice we want.

I liked the title, but then we changed it because we thought it had a sexual connotation. We changed it to "What Triggers Your Snack Button?" The personal anecdote in the lede is good, but it didn't influence me at all. We don't use a lot of anecdotes in our articles anyway unless they're about a fitness competitor or model.

The women-on-the-street anecdotes were also good, but we never did use any of them. Because of the magazine's niche being the fitness competitors, if there were any anecdotes, it would be from them. That's what makes our magazine different from the other ones.

The examples Beverly gave were awesome — they showed how professional she is. It's not that the idea was that original — you see it a lot in other magazines as well. It was that she had organized the article for me already. I knew exactly what I was getting. At that point I was looking for new writers as well, so I wasn't insecure about using Beverly.

Another thing Beverly does that a lot of other writers don't do is pitch regularly. I really got to learn what areas she could do. Even if a writer has already broken into a magazine, pitching is still a good idea. I'm always looking for more ideas — I only have my own.

USA Weekend

This writer uses celebrity sparkle to add panache to what otherwise might have been a plain vanilla fitness piece. Getting celeb quotes for a query is next-to-impossible for the average writer, so Tim Wendel did the next-best thing: He contacted the celeb's PR agent to verify information he'd found on the star's Web site.

Dennis:

Karl Malone works out five hours daily. And that's just what he does before lunch.

During the offseason, the 41-year-old power forward hits the gym from 7 a.m. to noon. He rarely takes a day off and in the afternoons he often does 40 minutes on the treadmill and a half-hour on the stationary bike before calling it a day.

"When I lineup against an opponent in the fourth quarter, I ask myself if this guy has paid the price I did," Malone says. "And I always come back and say, 'You know what, I could be wrong, but I don't think so.'"

Malone, along with football receiver Jerry Rice (42 next month) and slugger Barry Bonds (40), are proving that aging stars can still be elite athletes. They are also demonstrating how beneficial a quality exercise routine can be for the weekend warrior.

William Evans, author of "Biomarkers: The Ten Determinants of Aging You Can Control," says loss of muscle mass and endurance can be stabilized, even reversed, by following a vigorous regimen. That doesn't mean anybody has to be in the gym for hours, but Evans points out that strength in 100-year-olds was increased fourfold by lifting light weights. Recent studies also show that we get the most benefit from exercise if we do it at least 30 minutes a day, five to six days a week.

> Let's focus on Malone's workout routine and include several of these new findings about the power of staying fit.
>
> - Tim Wendel

The Writer: Tim Wendel

I teach writing at Johns Hopkins. One of the things I tell students when querying via e-mail is not to go on too long. I also tell them that you can be a bit more casual if you have at least a semblance of a relationship with the editor beforehand.

I was intrigued by the older athletes who are still doing pretty well. I just had to find out what they were doing. To get the quotes from Malone, I found information about his workout on his Web site. I didn't talk to Malone directly, but talked to his agent to make sure I was going down the right track. If you can't get the person himself, get someone you can run the information by.

There's a fair amount of research in this query. That's the toughest thing to nail down — you have an idea, but you need to take the extra step to get the research. I think it's important to get quotes — to a point. It makes the query more legit, but it can be a fine line. You don't want to be doing tons of research for a query somebody may not buy (even though it sure helps sell it). Also, you have to be careful that anybody you talk to early on realizes that the piece may or may not happen.

The Editor: Dennis McCafferty, Senior Writer

Tim's a known commodity with us, so obviously that doesn't hurt. But even if this was coming from someone I didn't know, I'd say it's good because he's got a theme here and it's tight. A lot of people feel you have to write a huge query, and magazines like *Ladies' Home Journal* expect you to practically write the whole story in the query. I don't feel that way. I've had people get stuff approved that came from one or two sentences. I'm just looking for a good idea.

Query Letters that Rock

The query was brief and to the point and the "it" factor was there immediately. I can't define the "it" factor, but I know it when I see it. You also have to get the cadence of our writing — the way we just feel. You can't write a *New Yorker*-y piece for us.

You don't need to bother getting quotes for your query; I wouldn't ask a writer to waste his or her time that way. Their time is money. Just give us a sense of who you would use. Besides, with ProfNet [www.profnet.com], finding people to interview is easy.

What Tim is saying in this query is, "Let's take one aspect of Karl Malone and make it applicable and relevant even to people who don't watch basketball." Tim's idea is to tell what can we learn from Karl Malone about his workout — to take pieces of what Karl Malone does. We've done the same thing with other athletes; we even did it with a NASCAR driver named Mark Martin who's a fitness freak.

I like that he brought in Jerry Rice and Barry Bonds because it gives us different ways to do this. We could do all three, and it would make a great cover story. If one of them had a Roger Clemens-type season, we would have entertained that possibility, but that just didn't work out. But what Tim delivered was still a great idea for a full-page feature.

I think the independent writer places far too much emphasis on the pitch. The reason some writers don't get assignments from us again is the follow through. They have a great pitch and great credentials, and their follow-through is awful. We're not a thick glossy like *Vanity Fair*, but there's still a high level of thought that goes into it. I've had some writers turn in stuff that's really sloppy. We'll find the names of people quoted misspelled, or the writer will have references to volcanoes that place them on the wrong side of Washington state. Just sloppy.

It's offputting when a writer is pushy and thinks getting a story based on a so-so idea is a lock and wants to know why he or she isn't getting assigned. Pitches too often sound like every story that's been covered to death by newspapers, with no creative spin for a magazine like ours. And the tried and true pet peeve is that the writer has no idea what works for the magazine, yet the writer is convinced that he or she knows exactly what works for the magazine.

And, oh, yeah, we're not *USA Today*. Don't get me wrong. I love *USA Today*. I read it every day and think it's always doing fantastic things — breaking big news and providing terrific money, sports, and life coverage with strong enterprise stories. But we're an entirely different product with a different need for tone and content. So, that said, we shouldn't be pitched as if we were *USA Today* with respect to lead times and story approaches.

Parenting

A writer will often come to an editor with a good idea, but what can set a good idea apart from a great idea is structure, as this query by writer Melody Warnick shows. Give the editor something she can hang your story on — a clever hook or a description of how you'll organize the piece — and she'll fall at your feet with tears of gratitude streaming from her eyes. Okay, we're exaggerating — she'll simply call you with an assignment. Money's way better than having somebody prone at your feet — unless you've got superiority issues.

Dear Sarah:

Welcome to Toddler Town:
5 Fun Ways to Boost Your Child's Fun Play

Sarah Smith, Articles Editor: I like that Melody's given me a headline and a dek. Although I probably wouldn't use it, it's cute and it gets the story across in a few words. It means there's potential for this story to be packaged. Stories that are big ideas are hard sells — if you can't explain your idea in ten words or less, it means I'm probably going to pass.

Imitation may not always seem like the sincerest form of flattery, especially when your 2-year-old's idea of playing mommy is to give her stuffed Tigger a time-out. But for a toddler, acting like the adults in her life — by chatting on a toy phone, driving a pretend car or bottle-feeding a baby — is a natural way to flex make-believe muscles. And it's not all fun and games, according to Doris Bergen, PhD, a professor of educational psychology at Miami University in Ohio, who says pretend play helps kids learn problem-solving skills and self-control.

Smith: Melody sounds like a mom in the trenches. She

either knows that Parenting *loves that sort of voice, or she just has it naturally. This sounds like a* Parenting *story to me. It's a little wry. She's not sarcastic, but she's not super earnest, either. It feels real and friendly. I'm getting her voice right away, and that's huge!*

As I read further along, I see there's more to the story. She's not only got the voice, but she's getting the developmental benefits of pretend play, the information a busy mom wants, right away.

In "Welcome to Toddler Town: 5 Fun Ways to Boost Your Child's Pretend Play," I'll help your readers create mini imagination stations where kids from 12 months to 3 years old can imitate the grown-up world they see every day — and stimulate their creativity while they do it. Consider these ideas:

Special Delivery Post Office — 12 months

What you need: A few days' worth of junk mail and 3-4 shoeboxes.

What you do: Place a shoebox in the door of each bedroom in your house. Then fill a small tote with a stack of credit card offers and catalogs and let your 1 year old hand-deliver a few to each mailbox. When she reaches the end of her route, she can gather the mail back up again. To add to the fun, let your toddler stamp some of the letters with stickers. Bonus: it may buy you some time while you pay the bills!

What your child learns: Not only will your little one get in some good walking practice, she'll beef up her hand-eye coordination.

To Market, To Market — 18 months

What you need: A basket, empty cereal and cracker boxes (stuff them with newspaper and tape the tops shut), and small cans, like tomato paste.

What you do: To create your grocery store, help your 18 month old line up the cans and packages on a low bookshelf. Then tell him he's in charge of dinner. While your toddler chooses what he wants, ask for mandarin oranges and see if he can pick them out of the line-up. Or invite him to arrange boxes and cans from biggest to smallest. After he's done shopping, he can use his pretend food to make dinner for his dolls.

What your child learns: Finally getting to choose exactly what he wants at the grocery store boosts your 18 month old's decision-making skills and self-confidence. Plus, sorting packages teaches him about shape, color and size.

Smith: This section shows she has strong structure for her story. For someone who hasn't written for us before, getting this in the query is crucial. I'm not going to take the time to read through an idea that has no structure and come up with one myself. I'm already doing that all day long on stories I already know I want to pursue. Writers have to convince me of two things: the topic AND the approach.

In this quick-read, graphics-driven article, I'll also tell parents how to create a pretend pet shop for a 2 year old, an ice cream parlor for a 2 and a half year old and a laundromat for a 3 year old. To make the feature even more fun, "Welcome to Toddler Town" can be laid out like a real town, with photos of children next to a quick description of the activity. For the "What Your Child Learns" section, I'll talk to child development experts like Bergin; Jerome Singer, professor of psychology at Yale University; and Edward Hallowell, author of "The Childhood Roots of Adult Happiness."

Smith: It can be hard for writers to think visually because they're so word centered. Melody suggests a couple ways to lay out the story, which is fine, though I often ignore suggestions like that because we work on the layout with the in-house art department. These kind of directives from a writer don't sway me either way.

More important is to provide a lot of entry points for the reader, which this pitch does. If one part of the story isn't as compelling, there's another point she can enter. If you have clever ideas for subheads, it shows me you've thought about how the reader can use the story. We may not use those exact subheads, but it really helps us see how the story works.

I'm the mom of a 2 year old and have written for Pregnancy, ePregnancy, ParentStages.com, Pregnancy-Today.com and Pregnancyand-Baby.com, among other publications. I'd be happy to send along clips, if you'd like.

I hope we can work together on "Welcome to Toddler Town."

Best,
Melody

The Writer: **Melody Warnick**

I got this idea from seeing an ad in a parenting magazine for one of those toy mailboxes — you know, made of plastic, costs $30 — and I thought you could totally make one yourself. It sparked this idea that the purpose of the toy was to urge your child to play pretend, to boost his imagination, so why spend $30 for that? You could create your own pretend mailbox, grocery store, ice cream shop and more. When the idea came together in my head, I felt confident that this was a story I could sell.

When I sent this query in to *Parenting*, I was at the beginning of my career. It was one of the first queries I circulated to a national magazine. I'd taken a class on query writing, and this was one of the ideas I'd worked on in the class. The teacher who runs the course urged me to include the Tigger example in the first paragraph to make the query seem more friendly and approachable. I included a hed and dek because I'd seen other writers do this with their query letters that sold — it just seemed like a good idea. I also read the magazine and noticed how they set up stories, so I thought it made sense to follow a similar structure in my query.

This wasn't the first query I'd sent to *Parenting*; I'd sent a few others. I checked with other writers who'd gotten into *Parenting*, and they said it had taken them 10 or 15 tries before they got an assignment, so that was my strategy … to keep pitching ideas until something came through. Around the time this story was assigned by Sarah, a couple other of my ideas I'd had circulating there got assigned, so it ended up being a good strategy!

Today I work with a lot of different editors at the magazine, and sometimes they come to me with stories. That's a really nice feeling! When you have to query, that marketing time cuts down on your hourly rate. I do like having the control when I write up my own queries, but it's really cool when I can skip that step.

The Editor: Sarah Smith, Articles Editor

Melody's pitch is perfect. She has broken the idea down into clever ideas that are easy to do. She clearly gets both the magazine and being a mom — it really comes through in this query. When this query was passed on to me by another editor, I probably read the first couple paragraphs, skimmed the first tip, then passed it to the other editors, all of whom thought Melody's activities and writing were clever. I don't even think I got to the end of this query because I didn't need to — I was sold in the first few paragraphs.

I e-mailed Melody and told her we loved her idea, but we wanted it as a short. I asked her to do four games, as tight as possible, without losing the tone. She was happy and thrilled to make these changes. A big plus. A new-to-me and a new writer fall into the same category with me — you never know what the deal is until you work with them, which is why I usually assign Ages + Stages pieces before features. Any writer who hasn't written for us is "new." I know it can be frustrating for some writers who've written for a lot of magazines, but the strong, professional writers quickly prove themselves. Right away you can tell if someone is going to be pleasant to work with, or if they're going to fight every suggestion.

The assignment went well. Some of the quotes were a little stilted, but we ironed those out. Melody still writes Ages + Stages for us, and does a lot of other department pieces and features. She's got a great tone and clever ideas, and those are what carry her. She now writes for other editors here at *Parenting*, and everyone loves her. When a writer does great work, her name does get passed around to other editors.

West

(Los Angeles Times Magazine)

Feeelings ... nothing but feeeeelings. Oh. Ahem. Excuse me. What we're trying to say is that in your queries, you need to let your feelings come across. Does your subject matter make you feel angry? Sad? Elated? Let that come through in your writing. If you can't whip up any emotion about your subject matter, why would your readers — or an editor? Of course, you may not want to turn in a tear-stained query about the third-quarter profits at the local cracker factory, but if your subject moves you, let it all hang out.

Dear Marty,

A Las Vegas developer named David Lispon came to the Last Best Place a few years ago and liked what he saw. Last year he dropped a huge garish guest ranch into an unspoiled Montana valley. Then he proclaimed that he was trademarking the phrase the "Last Best Place" for the exclusive use of his resort.

The response was fire-breathing outrage. The Last Best Place was the title of a collection of stories by Montana writers, coined in 1988 by Bill Kittredge, a gruff professor of English who edited the book. Montanans adopted it, the same way that Bud Guthrie's book The Big Sky was adopted, and served as a nickname for a generation.

The governor denounced Lipson, as did both Senators. Then a few weeks ago Montana's Senator Conrad Burns attached a rider to a bill forbidding the Copyright office from using any federal money to register the trademark. The issue is dead. But the skirmish points up a much bigger point — the American West as we knew it is over.

The Rocky Mountain West was a moment in time as much as a place. It was a high country brigadoon, hidden away by distance and climate and lack of jobs from the "real world." The hall marks were reasonably sized towns in a drop dead beautiful environment with the best of old fashioned values. There were rednecks, to be sure, but at least they wore cowboy hats.

The wave of settlement that began in the 1960s and 1970s were enough for the West. The new comers brought good restaurants and espresso and art films, along with an environmental sensibility. Now, however the boom is on like never before. The rush this time is for something economists call "amenities."

People are retiring, or have inherited money from their parents or are bringing jobs with them to live in a place where cities are small, the traffic light, and nearby mountains offer fishing and skiing and hiking. They are often making these places over with their idea of what the place should be; not necessarily what it is. The five fastest growing states in the country are part of the Third Coast.

The migration has this region convulsed with fundamental change. Cities and towns are grappling with rampant growth. Housing prices have soared. Environmental problems are legion. Near Cody, Wyoming, for example, new homes are eating up grizzly bear habitat. Millionaires from Ted Turner to Paul Allen of Microsoft are locking up huge ranches, taking the land from locals, breaking down the rural fabric. The West was famously egalitarian: the boom has created an "us and them" society.

And it is destroying the environment. I want to write about how sprawl is choking out the wildlife that people came to live with, how growth is causing a blight on the scenery they came to enjoy, and how thousands of newcomers are clogging the roads they loved because they were traffic-free.

Based on these things, and my experience as an easterner who came west in 1976 and stayed, I want to write a thoroughly reported essay with a point of view: the latest rush to the Third Coast is destroying the Last Best Place.

Jim

The Writer: Jim Robbins

The Last Best Place issue, that we are ruining a natural paradise by moving there, is the biggest environmental issue in the West, yet it hasn't been written about much.

I like to do stories that aren't formulaic and that haven't been done by someone else. Having lived and reported here for so long, I know what the stories are that aren't being done. It helps to have an expertise — mine is environmental stories — and to be able to find a strong narrative to tell those stories.

My queries are short and sharp. There's a saying in journalism: "Don't let the facts get in the way of a good story." That's important with a query. You want to write a good query and don't worry too much about the facts. You don't want to make facts up and misrepresent the story, but the goal is to really grab the editor and then worry about the facts when you're writing the piece.

I don't do a lot of research for a query; I just find a compelling story and pitch it in a compelling way. When you write the story, then you do the research and worry about what's right and what's not right.

I don't think you need to use a lot of quotes in the query...just get to the heart of what you want to do in three to five paragraphs. If I have a great quote I'll use it, but if not I won't.

I might write a longer query if it's a cold query and the editor doesn't know me, but for editors who are already familiar with my work, a shorter query works fine.

The Editor: **Martin J. Smith, Senior Editor**

We're defined as a magazine of California and the West and we're always looking for stories that say something about the particular western mindset. Half the stories we run are about the struggle for resources. That's what Jim pitched, but in a new and different format. He had staked his claim, but was willing to go out on a limb and say, "But don't *you* come." Here's this guy who's willing to say, "I got mine, but you're not going to get yours if I have anything to do with it." That's very provocative. We're looking for stories that make people think.

Jim understands our audience very well. For the most part, our readers came here from somewhere else, whether it's Central America or central Pennsylvania. He understands what California is and what resonates here. That was the biggest thing this pitch had going for it.

This query had the two elements we're looking for: voice and place. The place in this case is the American West. This is one of those classic Western frontier stories.

Until three months ago, this magazine was in the model of *The New York Times Magazine,* with outside-in stories where a writer goes into a topic and explores it and then comes out again and explains it. We've had a fundamental shift in what the magazine is looking for; we're now looking for inside-out stories that start with the writer's point of view. This is a good example of an inside-out story ... he's angry and he's feeling like his wide-open space is being invaded. He takes it personally when someone from Los Angeles buys the biggest house in Helena, Montana, and blows everybody else's property values out of whack.

What you see here is a revised pitch. What Jim pitched first was a story about the migration of Californians to Montana. But we're not doing those stories anymore. I told him, "If this is disrupting your life, tell us how and why it makes you angry."

Once we talk these things through, I'll have two to three hours of conversation with the writer before we even write an assignment letter. When we put it down on paper, we're asking for something very specific.

American Profile

Blah, blah, blah. Get to the point! You may think that editors want to read pages and pages of your beautiful prose, but really what they want is this: They want to know what the heck it is you're proposing to do for them. What editor Richard McVey liked most about this query is that it let him know right off what the writer wanted to do (profile a company that makes washboards) and what makes the idea special (the company is the country's only remaining manufacturer of washboards). No thought-provoking imagery about bygone eras, no flowery phrases designed to make the editor all teary-eyed with nostalgia. Just solid information that answers all of the editor's questions about the topic.

Dear Mr. McVey:

In these modern days of technological conveniences, it's hard to imagine a time when people washed their clothes by hand. Regardless, washboards are still being manufactured, and they generally have two markets — the Amish who still use them for their intended purpose and the home furnishings and craft market where they are appreciated for their quality design. Still, it's a big enough market to keep the Columbus Washboard Company operational. Located in Logan, Ohio, it is the country's only remaining manufacturer of washboards.

I would like to propose an article for AMERICAN PROFILE about the Columbus Washboard Company, including its rich history and the company tours where visitors can see the washboards being made firsthand. The washboards come in a variety of styles, and most boards are made from Ohio-grown white pine and tulip poplar. In addition, woodcrafters have transformed these tools into cabinets, magazine racks, coffee tables and other types of furniture, while musicians have been known to use them as percussion instruments for jazz and rhythm and blues. Washboards are available for purchase on site or by mail, ranging in price from $14 to $24, and admission to the tour is free.

It should be noted that recent washboard shipments to U.S. troops overseas have heightened the awareness of this pioneer-like product. The company is proud to be sending shipments of laundry supplies to help the troops, and donations are being accepted for this cause. Information about this opportunity, as well as tips on how to use a washboard, might make a good sidebar.

As far as my writing qualifications are concerned, my work has appeared in several publications, including Ohio Magazine, Midwest Living, American Way (American Airlines), Woman's Day, Cleveland Plain Dealer Sunday Magazine, Parents, Family Fun, Traverse, Cape Cod Life and Country Living. Clips are enclosed for your convenience.

Sincerely,
Lori B. Murray

The Writer: Lori Murray

I write regularly for *Ohio Magazine,* so I'm in tune with things going on here. As I started thinking about doing something for *American Profile,* I thought, "What do I know here in Ohio?" I had done a big piece for *Ohio* magazine called the Heritage Driving Tour, where I write one-paragraph blurbs on places that have a historical significance in Ohio; the Columbus Washboard Company had appeared in this.

Plus, at the time I pitched this, we were getting involved in Iraq and the Columbus Washboard Company was shipping their washboards overseas so the troops could wash their clothes.

I'm still trying to figure out whether it's best to come up with an idea and then find a market for it or to choose a magazine and think of ideas for it. It's probably more profitable to have a great idea and find a magazine for it, but for this query that wasn't the case. I just thought it would be fun to write for *American Profile*.

I spoke with someone at the company before writing the query. I usually tell people straight up that I'm doing preliminary research on a possible article for such-and-such magazine. Usually people are pretty good about it. And certainly, with a place like the Columbus Washboard Company, they're excited about the possibility of getting some publicity.

Sometimes I begin my queries with an anecdote, but this idea didn't lend itself to that. The style is very straightforward. I wanted to get out the facts — there was a lot of information I wanted Richard to know about. One of the things I feel that I need to work on in my queries is that sometimes I wait too long to make my point. I need to make the point very early on in the query.

Sometimes with a first query I pitch via mail; that was the case here, though every correspondence I've had since has been through e-mail. I also have my clips online as PDF files for when I query via e-mail.

My tip to writers is to keep on querying. That's how you stay in business. I've set a goal for the number of queries and follow-ups I do. You have to just stick with it.

The Editor: Richard McVey, Editor

I'd say that fewer than 10 percent of the queries we get work for us, and the majority of those are from writers who are already established with us. But Lori's query got what we were about. It had a positive slant to it, which is something our magazine does well. We do positive, uplifting human interest-type stories where we look at the good things in life and offer up a slice of Americana.

Lori did a great job of pointing out what made this particular company unique. We wouldn't just do a story on someone who makes fill-in-the-blank. Lori mentioned that the Columbus Washboard Company is America's only remaining manufacturer of washboards. She also did a good job right off the bat of answering the basic question: Who's buying washboards these days?

Something else we try to do is look at history and tie it to modern day. In the second paragraph, Lori said the article would include the history of the company as well as information about what the company is doing today. The query even finished off with a patriotic slant with the information about the U.S. troops. She gave me so many different angles to approach this from, it was difficult to say no.

We look for timeless stories. If you send us something with a quick news hook, we can't use it. We're working months out on a lot of these features. The information about the troops was as time-sensitive as it could get.

The query jumped right into the pitch. I hate it when I have to keep going and going to get to the point. I don't have time to read a page before I figure out what the writer wants to do. And sometimes I get too little information in a query, which leaves me scratching my head. Lori's query was straightforward and clean, and it answered all my questions. Our feature stories have to be concise, informative, and engaging. When I'm reading a query, I'm looking for those same qualities.

Sometimes a pitch may be so generic that you read it and you're not quite sure what the hook is. What makes the idea unique? If Lori didn't mention that the Columbus Washboard Company was the only remaining manufacturer of washboards in the country, I would have asked, why is this unique? Include details that make the idea special. Don't tell me there's a town in Tennessee that holds a festival every year. So? There are hundreds of towns in Tennessee that have a festival. I want to know what makes this festival unique. You have to tell me enough information in the query to say why your idea stands out.

The best thing you can do is read several issues of the magazine and know what we're about. We have headings on our feature stories, such as Hometown Heroes. If you can focus the angle of your story so it fits one of our headings, it says you understand what we're all about. Some writers notice that in the Hometown Spotlight, we often interview the mayor and always quote residents, and I occasionally get a query that says, "I'd like to interview the mayor and several residents." That shows you know the magazine. The more a query resembles what we do in our magazine, the better.

Inc.

Think when you assume the glorious position of contributing editor at a magazine you can sit back and let your editors feed you story ideas? Writer Alison Stein Wellner is a contributing editor at *Inc.* magazine, yet she still brings ideas to her editors and writes proposals for her stories — incredibly well written and researched proposals that have her editors begging for more. If you're just starting out, Alison's proposal is a model you can strive for. And if you're already at the top of your game, learn the secrets of how another pro sells her work.

Larry:

At the age of 20, Gary Heavin, a down-on-his luck med school drop out, decided to acquire a failing gym in Houston, Texas. He turned it into a huge success, and quickly found another location in the area, and then another, and then another, so within 10 years, he was running a mini-fitness empire: 17 locations.

This, however, is not where the Curves story begins. Soon after Heavin opened the 17th location, the entire business crumbled and shut down — Heavin has since attributed the failure to too-rapid expansion.

In 1992, Heavin launched Curves, and his second venture has been a bit more successful than the first. The stats are familiar — four million members, one Curves location for every two McDonald's in the United States and so on.

What's interesting to me is that Heavin might again be at a place (albeit at a far larger scale) where he faces the risk of too-rapid, or maybe misguided expansion. The company is rapidly pushing into the international market, which will pose a whole new set of challenges, and, in what's possibly brilliant, but seems to me a puzzling move, into the troubled travel agency business. This year, the company is offering trip planning and booking services to Curves members. The company's equity is obviously in fitness and weight loss, but they think their equity is with women, and therefore will be equally powerful with travel as with things relating to weight loss and exercise. It's hard to say right now whether this is brilliant or boneheaded.

This story would of course need to look at how Curves got to where it is today — it's incredibly difficult to communicate with consumers about weight/fitness issues, much less do so effectively on a national basis, you can count the number of national fitness chains on one hand. I'd like to mostly focus on the crossroads the company is facing right now: how you take a company that's become a behemoth and make it continue to grow, when your company is at the point where it seems like it has no where to go but down? After all, the market is fairly saturated, competitors are nipping at your heels, and fourteen years is a long time in the faddish fitness market. I think the second most difficult time to grow a company is when the company has grown so much that you have to push out in a different direction. (The first is right at the beginning.) Curves is definitely right at that point, and while most *Inc.* readers aren't looking at the scale of success that Curves has had, I think they'll be able to relate to the strategic decisions that Heavin faces.

As I said on the phone the other day, I think that it would be interesting to pair this story up with a sidebar on the obesity crisis/opportunity. (And with that one sentence, I will probably have to resign my liberal card and purchase my one-way ticket to hell.) Nearly two-thirds (64%) of Americans are overweight or obese, this costs more than $150 billion a year. This is for the most part a bad thing for *Inc.* readers, who will pay for

> a big chunk of that $150 billion via health insurance premiums, but it's also a big opportunity for any company that can find a way to even just chip away at the problem. This has created something of a gold rush, for a huge range of companies, ranging from biotechs to companies that sell in-home fitness DVDs. I thought it could be fun to profile a few of these companies that are making in-roads and discuss where the opportunities are in this obesity thing, where the pitfalls are, and so on.
>
> Alison

The Writer: Alison Stein Wellner

A couple years ago, Larry and I met for coffee to talk about some things I might write for the magazine and he said, "Curves." I added the idea to my list, but honestly, I was only a little interested at the time. Larry did send me news clippings about Gary Heavin and his company, which I filed away. We moved on to other stories.

In the two years since Larry and I spoke, Heavin became big in the news over his controversial political views. I knew the story I wrote for *Inc.* wouldn't be about his politics, but it jogged my memory about the conversation I'd had with Larry all those years ago. I knew that writing just about Curves, as a company, wouldn't be enough for *Inc.* I'd have to find an angle and an approach. Now, I often write about health and healthcare, and I'd been wanting to write about the obesity epidemic and the way it's playing out for fast-growing companies for a while. It occurred to me one Sunday morning while reading the paper that the story about Curves would be an interesting way to explore the obesity epidemic, while telling the story of an interesting entrepreneur and his company. I called Larry on Monday and asked him if he was still interested in a story on Curves, and he was. He asked me to write up a pitch.

I wanted a big feature with a lot of space, so I knew I had to sell this. Even though I'm a contributing editor at *Inc.*, if I want the real estate in the magazine, I have to sell a clear vision of a compelling story. This meant doing some research ahead of time, giving myself the assignment before I had the assignment. Doing some initial research gets everyone on the same page, so that when I get the assignment, I'm not sitting there saying, "Now what?" Also, sometimes I don't have a lot of time to report and write. The minute Larry gave me the green light, I was on the phone with Curves' PR instead of sitting at my desk trying to figure out an angle.

Inc. could probably keep me busy writing their own ideas, and they have come to me with some great ones. But I usually find my own ideas more interesting, and so that means that I need to pitch my own ideas. I don't often get assignments on the strength of a sentence, and to be honest, I don't think I'd want that to happen. With a story proposal, I get to describe something that doesn't exist, laying the story out and exciting the person who's going to fund it. With all creative professions there's an equivalent. Behind every great painting, the artist has done studies of his subject. Industrial designers have their sketch models. Writers have their proposals. Editors are not out to get us when they ask for proposals; they're the heavy creative lifting we need to do to tell a story well.

The Editor: Larry Kanter, Articles Editor

I met Alison when I was working at *BusinessWeek*. She freelanced there, and when I moved over to *Inc.*, she continued writing for me. She quickly became a go-to person because she's always curious, an unusually good writer, and someone who's good to brainstorm with. Another great thing about Alison is that she's an idea machine. It's hard for editors to come up with good ideas all the time. If the well is running dry, I can call Alison and say, "I need story ideas for Hands On" [one of *Inc.'s* departments]. One of the most important things for us is a writer who is bringing good stuff to the magazine, not a writer who is waiting for an assignment. We have plenty of talented freelancers on hand who can write.

With this Curves pitch, Alison is clearly well informed and knows what she's talking about. I've got a pretty good idea of what the story will say, where it's going, what the point of view will be. You can see Alison's a terrific reporter; the research started before she got the assignment. She doesn't hit the send button too early and she won't send me a half-baked idea. We get a lot of pitches where the writer asks to go on a fishing expedition. What impresses me with a pitch letter is when I can see the person has done some homework and they know what they're going to say.

For example, what I would have seen in an unsuccessful pitch for this idea would be the stats, which would be summed up with, "We should do a story about their CEO." When you read Alison's pitch, however, she shows Heavin is in a place where he could become misguided. There's drama and tension, a forward spin to the story. You can see where Heavin is heading, and it makes you wonder if he's going in the right direction or is he poised to make a huge mistake.

Alison's suggested sidebar is yet another example of how she's an idea machine. It's probably not something we're going to do, but it shows she's always thinking. You can also see that Alison's witty. Some people are wittier than others, but even a little bit of wit and personality goes far in a good pitch letter. It shows me you have some voice, that you bring something to the story.

I have some freelancers who work for me constantly. They're not the best writers, but they're so good at coming up with ideas, it's worth it for me to keep them in the fold. They bring in expertise we don't have in-house. So it's not just coming up with some great writing; it's answering the question, How can I best help solve the needs of this magazine? It comes from understanding who we are. A lot of writers think of us as a "small business magazine" so they'll say, "Here's a story about a small business owner." They don't take the time to get *Inc.'s* voice and what we're trying to accomplish. Our stories give guidance to business owners and help them run a growing company. The Curves story is something a small business owner can learn from.

El Restaurante Mexicano

Who's the expert? You are! Here's a query where the writer's expertise in the proposed topic is what impressed the editor the most. You may start out your writing career as a generalist, but as you begin to develop niches you should work to become a specialist in those areas. In this case, not only does writer Kathryn Cordova run a business in the food industry, but she reads up on news and advances in nutrition, restaurant management, and other foodie topics.

Dear Ms. Kathleen Furore:

While I am an enthusiastic reader of your upbeat & useful magazine, El Restaurante Mexicano, I think I can offer you a timely article I've researched and written on those controversial Trans Fats. One article in your March-April 2004 issue entitled "Mexican Restaurants capitalize on the low-carb craze" touched a bit upon the need for low fat diets among some hispanics with a higher rate of diabetes. Today, the new focus on Zero Trans Fats in fried foods is my topic due to the January, 2006 change in the FDA's labeling laws now facing retail outlets—with foodservice not far behind.

Attached is a piece I wrote for the New Mexico Restaurant Association.

It was just published in their bimonthly magazine, Southwest Restaurateur. Since your audience is national in scope and targets the hispanic restaurants, I can tailor my slant to fit your magazine's requirements. Please let me know if you can fit my article idea into either of your new columns, "Taking on Technology" or "Healthy Menu Ideas" or as a feature. Thank you for considering this.

Your sincere reader,
Kathy Cordova

Query Letters that Rock

The Writer: Kathryn Cordova

Often my article ideas come from my current business connections in food product marketing and sales. My husband and I own the last operating family-owned flour mill in our state. We invented a way to make traditional sopaipillas in a healthy way with our "just-add-water" mix. I read food ingredient and nutrition magazines constantly. Recently, I made a self-study of edible fats — especially monounsaturates, polyunsaturates, saturates and trans fats (the worst kind for cardiovascular health!). In the case of my query letter to *El Restaurante Mexicano,* I knew that a previous article I'd written on Zero Trans Fats product development including a survey of new ZT vegetable oils on the market was timely for most food magazines.

My first copy of *El Restaurante Mexicano* magazine came from a current restaurant customer of ours because he thought we could learn more about our Mexican restaurant marketplace. He was right; I've been a subscriber for over a year now. Every month I find valuable food trends and other information in this magazine; as a result, I'm already familiar with the magazine's subject matter.

Although I have one year's worth of *El Restaurante Mexicano's* issues in my office for reference, I wanted to see how often the editor ran stories on dietary fat or fried foods. So I went online to the magazine site and explored some past issues. My research led me to conclude that the "Healthy Menus" column or perhaps another new column might fit my topic. To understand the editorial direction and goals of the magazine in communicating with its readership, I read some of Kathleen's "Editor's Note" columns. These are basically sales techniques to learn more about your potential customer — then you're better prepared to make your sales pitch, which is the query letter.

Sometimes I will include an expert quote in a query, but more frequently I'll just mention an expert if I have an interview planned with him or her. Most of my queries don't rely on another expert's quote because I plan to offer the magazine editor a new perspective on a timely topic. I prefer to offer news, not a rewrite of others' information. Once I write the feature article I use both quotes and expert resources to establish the authority and credibility of the information I present.

Query Letters that Rock

My salutation included both the editor's first and last name, but I don't remember why I did it this way…perhaps I was identifying with her name, which is similar to mine. Her name is another form of Kathryn, also with a K. Perhaps it was because I was studying her editorial and that's how her name appears there. But I would not use an informal, first name address in my first query to an editor whom I don't know personally. That implies casual presumption and is inappropriate in a business letter.

Query letters should be short. Editors are busy people; to get their attention your writing should be short and to the point. Respect their time and deadlines. In this case, because I was planning to use my basic research from a previously published article, I simply added that article as an attachment to my e-mail query letter. That reduced the need to quote from my article. Instead, Kathleen could refer to the attachment after reading my proposal to modify and slant an article for *El Restaurante Mexicano's* readers. When Kathleen replied to my query she asked me to select a New Mexican restaurant using our product and frying it in a Zero Trans fat oil. Very quickly she and I were able to reshape my original article into a new column to fit her editorial needs.

The format I used for my attached clip was a jpeg image because there were three photos included in the article that supported the written text. By sending my entire article with photos, I was trying to establish myself as a photojournalist who would be able to include an original photo for the new article I was querying. Also, the size of the file I attached was large enough for the editor to easily read and assess the quality of my work.

Many writers want to break into food and restaurant writing. To succeed, it's vital to master the subject matter by studying, not just reading, periodical literature and references in the companion fields of foods and nutrition, business management of restaurants, food processing, food industries, baking, culinary arts, recipe and menu development, and food trends. That is a tall order. I'm fortunate to be part of the food industry and therefore a player in some of these markets. But, in my opinion, an individual with cooking experience who watches television food shows or reads food industry literature can develop sufficient background to write for food and restaurant magazines.

Query Letters that Rock

Breaking into freelancing for the specialty magazines for restaurants and foods will involve some library or Internet research to discover niche markets. Most industry or trade magazines have small editorial staffs, so if a writer can establish an expertise to cover as a contributing writer or reporter for pay, that's a good start. Hospitals often have patient newsletters and may welcome freelance topics on healthy foods or special diets. Look for small, specialized publications at first and write your very best. Definitely use your computer to spell check and proofread your copy before submitting either a query letter or the finished article. The national magazines are more difficult to break into until a writer is seasoned and has clips of published work.

Spend your time researching a few newsworthy topics on foods or food trends. Next, compose a query that will grab the busy editor's interest and if possible fit an urgent need! The urgency may be that your location is costly for the magazine to travel to and you're already on the scene. Maybe you have a chef friend with a new invention or theme restaurant in a major city. Select the magazine carefully so that your topic is within their "slant." Only by carefully reading several issues of a magazine can you discover the slant and style and probable demographics of the readership. Researching the magazine's editorial slant is a key to writing an effective query letter that sells the editor on both you and your proposed topic.

The Editor: Kathleen Furore, Editor

I liked that Kathy's query was short and to the point. I have so little time to go through all my mail that the shorter and more to the point, the better.

The query showed she had read *El Restaurante Mexicano* and understood who our readers are. It can only help if the writer knows the publication they want to write for! E-mailing or writing to request a sample copy is a good idea (although I'll admit I get so busy that I sometimes forget to send the sample). Writers also can turn to a magazine's website for information about the publication. At www.restmex.com, for example, we explain who the magazine is for and include the full text of stories from past issues.

Kathy attached her clip as a jpeg image. I don't really have a preference for clip format. And to be honest, I rarely read clips thoroughly. If I see that a writer has experience and understands what we're about, I'm usually willing to give him or her a try. I know that clips can be deceiving, anyway. I can't tell how much the story has been edited, for example, or how many rewrites the writer was asked to do. Believe me, I've had to do some pretty heavy editing on some stories. If writers used those edited stories as clips, they wouldn't be representative of that writer's talent in the least!

Kathy mentions that she wrote a similar story for another magazine. I have extremely strong feelings on this. Writers should absolutely let the editor know if a story they're proposing has appeared in a competing magazine or if they are sending the same query to the competition. I had an incident in which one of my writers wrote a story for me and an almost identical story for my biggest competitor. Luckily, I got a copy of the competing magazine before my issue went to press and saw the article. I didn't run her story and never used her again. And I know some editors won't even use writers who write for competing magazines.

In Kathy's case, the magazine in which her story appeared was published by her state's restaurant association, so it wasn't really a competing publication. I also asked her to add quite a bit of information, so in the end it wasn't that similar to her original piece.

Kathy addressed me by first and last name ("Dear Ms. Kathleen Furore"), which is fine. I really don't care how someone addresses me as long as they take the time to find out my name. What I don't like is a letter that says, "Dear Editor," "Dear Madam," or "To Whom it May Concern."

As for credentials, Kathy did mention she had written for her state restaurant association publication, and demonstrated that she knew something about the foodservice industry, so I really didn't care about credentials beyond that. However, I think I'm more lenient than many editors on this (probably because I also own the magazine and only have myself and my business partner to answer to!). However, I also freelance, and some of the publications I write for were adamant about getting multiple clips that showed I had a strong knowledge of the topic they cover.

I don't expect the writers to include expert quotes in their queries. But it would impress me if they included the name or a source or two they planned to contact for the story.

My biggest pet peeve? Getting queries that show the freelancer has no idea whatsoever what *El Restaurante Mexicano* is about. I frequently get queries that are nothing more than restaurant reviews of a writer's favorite Mexican restaurant. They don't get it that our readers are owners, operators and chefs and not diners looking for the best margarita in town. Not far behind: Getting blast e-mail queries that have obviously been sent out to multiple publications.

NWA WorldTraveler

If you're afraid to pick up the phone and call an editor, reading the story of this query will cure you. Writer Ellise Pierce had such a hot topic, she called the magazine and pitched her idea over the phone. The query below is what she whipped off when the editor asked for a quick written description to show the rest of the magazine's staff. And the result of the phone call? An assignment with a national magazine to interview a famous (and hilarious) author in Paris.

SEDARIS IN PARIS

He has been called the country's pre-eminent humorist, and likened to Woody Allen, Evelyn Waugh, Mark Twain, and even Voltaire. His latest collection of essays, "Dress Your Family in Corduroy and Denim," has been on The New York Times bestseller list for 109 weeks. Over the last decade, David Sedaris has written four books; all collections of essays based on his hilarious, wildly dysfunctional childhood (to today); won the Thurber Prize for American Humor (2001); and now sells books by the truckload.

Now living in Paris, France, Sedaris got his start on NPR's "Morning Edition," when he told a story called "Santaland Diaries." Sedaris' true story of working as an elf at Macy's during the Christmas rush struck a chord with listeners — it became one of the most requested cassette recordings — and launched Sedaris into the sea of literary stardom.

Now a movie is in the works on Sedaris' life. My idea is to sit down with the normally reclusive writer, in Paris — or in his fixer-upper in Normandy, wherever he chooses — and find out what he's up to now, in a New Yorker "Talk of the Town" style. We could do a sidebar w/ an excerpt from his latest book, and another, with Sedaris'

---

favorite spots in Paris.

His books: "Barrel Fever," "Naked," "Me Talk Pretty One Day," "Dress Your Family in Corduroy and Denim."

The Writer: **Ellise Pierce**

I was in the process of putting together a list of stories I wanted to sell while I was in Paris for a month visiting my boyfriend. I didn't know who would want a David Sedaris story, but I thought, "Who wouldn't?" I had actually tried to get an interview with him in the spring of last year and couldn't get in touch with him. He has a PR flak through the publishing house as well as a guy who organizes his speaking tour, and they hadn't been encouraging me in any way to pursue a David Sedaris interview — but when fall rolled around I thought I'd try it again. I just wanted to meet him, I thought it would be a fun story, and it would be an opportunity to write something in the way I wanted to write it. I got the okay from the publicist at the publishing company. She said, "I can't believe it, but he's okay with this interview, and that's very rare." She promised to get back in touch closer to the date of the interview.

Since I was going to Paris, the airline magazines were an obvious market. Part of my research was to find out which airlines service Paris, and then which of those airline's magazines might want this story. Generally speaking, what you want to do is spend as much time up front researching the publication as possible so you know the publication as well as the editor, and you can say, "I've got a story idea for this section and this is why it's going to work." I knew about *NWA WorldTraveler* from what I'd seen of it online. They had Paris on their editorial schedule for a particular month, so I thought I'd pitch the idea there.

I was sitting here with a David Sedaris interview, and I needed to sell it and make sure it was a locked-down interview. I had never worked with the magazine before, and I just picked up the phone and called. This is how I've started a lot of relationships with editors. But I don't just call to tell them who I am — if I call, I'm going to have a story idea for them.

Query Letters that Rock

I reached Dobby and said, This is who I am, I'm spending a month in Paris, and I want to do a story on David Sedaris. He asked me to write up the idea, so I sent clips and followed up with this note. He passed it on to his editor and I got the cover story.

When I say in the query that I want to do the interview "Talk of the Town" style, it was because I didn't know how else I could do the story. David Sedaris is reclusive and quirky, so I knew it wouldn't be a typical sit-down Q&A style interview. It would have to be something really loose, just hangin' out with David. Normally I do a catchier query with a headline and four or five paragraphs, beginning in the same way I would start the article, but because I didn't know what I would get with Sedaris, this query is somewhat general.

Every day I try to think of ways to pitch Paris since I go there so often. Everybody knows Paris is a great city, so that idea itself won't work as a feature. Plus, there are already lots of American journalists living in Paris, so that works against me, too. It's a challenge. I've got to dig and research, and before that I have to research the magazines to know, for example, that at *Delta Sky* they want their stories to be like this, and at *NWA WorldTraveler* they want their stories to be like that. When you pitch your idea, it's got to look almost exactly like their copy looks — like a mini version of the story. That tells the editor that you're familiar with their magazine, that you've done your homework.

You can have a disastrous situation if you send a query that doesn't match anything in the magazine — the editor won't read the next one. So I've always felt that it makes sense to spend two or three days on a query, because in the end, I may make two or three thousand dollars on the assignment. I think that the key is to not just know the magazine's demographic and their particular format, but also try to think like an editor. Imagine if you were an editor of that publication. Would you really want the story that you're pitching? Sometimes after I write a query, I have second thoughts about it, and decide in the end, that it probably won't work for that publication. Knowing when to not send a query, I think, is as important as knowing when to send one.

Query Letters that Rock

The Editor: Dobby Gibson, Editorial Director

Ellise called out of the blue and two things made me pay attention: she had experience writing for *Texas Monthly*, and she said she had done the preliminary legwork toward an interview with David Sedaris, and she was prepared to fly to Paris to do it in person.

Sometimes when people call out of the blue I'm inclined not to pay attention because I get overwhelmed with calls. If you're calling, you better have a solid idea the way Ellise did. It's a bad idea to call an editor and look for an assignment without having something specific in mind. I'm surprised at how many freelance writers contact me without having anything to pitch. There are too many freelance writers in the world, and you're not going to rise to the top by saying, "I'm here and I'm a generalist." You have to bring something to the table.

It's okay to call if you've already sent an e-mail. It's easy to get lost in the backwash of spam in my inbox. But my suggestion would be to call after hours and leave a voicemail.

I asked Ellise to write something up so we could talk about it internally. I thought the query was great — it was really concise and zippy, and conveyed the idea of how fun it would be to hang out with David Sedaris. We then did a little back and forth in terms of firming up the scope of the story.

Ellise sounded really experienced and trustworthy—it didn't sound like she was just winging it. She had us convinced.

I was just doing a presentation to a group of travel writers, and I told them to try and defy conventional wisdom in some way. If the story idea sounds like something that would run on a Chamber of Commerce Web site, rethink it and find a fresh angle on your subject or destination. For example, if you pitch "Atlanta: Jewel of the New South," well, everyone's read that a zillion times. If you're going to write about Atlanta, maybe there are five new chefs who have opened 50-seat restaurants that are changing the dining landscape. There's so much travel writing being done now that you have to work a bit harder up front to come up with a different angle, and if you do that you'll really stand out.

My query pet peeve is rhetorical questions like "Did you ever wonder why...?" That's just window dressing. Cut to the chase. Whatever the next sentence after the question is, start with that.

One thing that works for me is freelance writer Web sites. I think those are great tools. I often bookmark them, and I'm more apt to go back and check them than I am to go back and check an e-mail. E-mail gets lost more easily. With a Web site you can put all your clips out there and show the broad range of what you do.

ATA World

(the magazine of the American Taekwondo Association)

Know thy market. Even though Susan Lennon had experience in taekwondo, she made sure to ask for copies of the magazine and then study them like she was going to be tested. Then she proved her familiarity with the magazine by conforming to its conventions in her query, such as writing taekwondo instead of tae kwon do and do-jahng instead of dojang.

We know, we know. As Renegades, we say that if you don't have access to a magazine but you're sure your idea is a great fit, pitch anyway. But this isn't an excuse to be lazy; if you can get your hands on a copy or two of the magazine, even if it means e-mailing to ask for copies, then do it.

Dear Jennifer,

A couple of months after I earned my first degree Black Belt, I broke my ankle and had a complicating blood clot. In a cast for 12 weeks, and on a blood-thinner for an additional eight, I couldn't imagine how I'd ever catch up. Worse, I worried that after all those months of forced inactivity, I'd lose my motivation.

But Taekwondo had taught me to be a problem-solver and a fighter. So I abandoned my defeatist thoughts and found ways to stay involved throughout my recovery — and three years later, I earned my second degree.

As Mr. Robert Ferguson, 6th degree Black Belt, author and motivational coach says, "A setback is simply a set-up for a comeback."

I'd like to write "8 Ways to Maintain Motivation While Recovering from an Injury" for ATA World.

In addition to using my own experience, I'll talk to sports psychology, motivational, and fit-

---

ness/martial arts experts like Patrick Cohn, PhD; Joseph J. Kolezynski, MBA, PhD; and others.

Practical and affirming tips will include:

1. Be physical in other ways (if you can't kick, punch, and vice versa) — I'll offer safety tips based on the type of injury
2. Hook up with someone else in your Do-Jahng who has an injury and drill together — I'll interview someone who has done this
3. Use visualization techniques to maintain your Black Belt attitude — I'll include several techniques
4. Listen to/read motivational works — I'll list Taekwondo and other resources
5. Meditate to stay in the moment — I'll offer tips from an expert
6. Read Taekwondo books and rent, borrow, buy videos — I'll provide suggestions
7. Go to your Do-Jahng at class time; observe as if you were the teacher — Mr. Ferguson describes "becoming your own instructor"
8. Work on Korean terminology — I will include motivational examples

I'll also add a sidebar for parents about how they can help their kids stay interested through coaching, working with the instructor, and setting small goals.

For a bit about me, I'm a Master's Level Licensed Clinical Social Worker and 2nd Degree Taekwondo Black Belt whose credits include Newsweek, The Washington Post, Health, USA Weekend Magazine, and others.

Thanks, Jennifer! I look forward to hearing back from you.

Best,

Susan

Query Letters That Rock

The Writer: Susan T. Lennon

I broke my ankle in 1997. I was laid up for a really long time — I had not only a broken ankle, but also a blood clot, and I couldn't be in a regular Taekwondo class for eight months because I couldn't get hit while I was on the medication. So I came up with things I could do outside of class to stay motivated and in shape. I thought my experience would be something other people could learn from.

I wrote and asked for samples of the magazine before pitching. They all have a certain way of describing things, and if you misspell terms they use, that's a tip-off that you don't know the magazine you're pitching.

I also needed to know how the magazine refers to people — first name, last name, Mr., etc. — and whether they use any first-person anecdotes in their articles, whether they use subheads, and whether they use bullets. It's always a good idea to write the query in the style of the magazine.

The PR person of one of my potential sources, Robert Ferguson, sent me his book, so I called him up and asked if he wanted to talk about my idea, and he gave me a great quote. I did some research on ProfNet to find more people who I thought would be both good martial arts and sports psychology experts, because I could tell from the magazine that it wasn't all first-person anecdotal. I talked with Ferguson on the phone, but the other ones I didn't talk to ... I just did some research to make sure they really existed. I always write, "I'll talk to experts like X, Y, and Z." I don't guarantee that specific sources will talk to me, unless I've already spoken with them.

The numbered points I put in the query were what I expected to put into the article. Generally speaking, I do this for all queries. If I'm going to propose ten tips, I often flesh out the first two or three and then say, "Other tips will include" and bullet point the others.

The Editor: Jennifer Lawler, Editor

With *ATA World*, if you just blindly query you will never get it — but it's not a magazine you can find on the newsstands. So it makes sense to do what Susan did, which is to write with an introduction and ask for copies (if you impress me with your letter of introduction, I'm more likely to send you copies). Once she had the material she was able to craft an appropriate query.

What I liked about this query was that it showed that she had personal experience in taekwondo, which is kind of important since this is a taekwondo magazine. She also queried an angle that she had personal experience in: that she hurt herself and had to recover, but didn't want to lose her motivation or stop training. That personal twist really helped draw me into the query.

But she didn't rely on her personal experience. Right away she introduced a sixth degree black belt/coach, which shows me that she understands she will have to use experts in her article, and that she's willing to do work to get the quotes. Then she gets into the specifics and gives ways to stay motivated. Susan has thought about how the article is going to flesh out, and she also knows who she's going to talk to.

I have people who want to write for the magazine who are very lazy about interviewing people. Because they practice martial arts, they want to write based only on their personal experience, and we can't use that kind of writing. It's important to show that you're willing to do those interviews.

Susan also showed that she understood the demographics of the magazine. The majority of people in the ATA are children, and she offered a sidebar for parents.

Susan closes with information about herself and who she's written for, which confirms to me that she can write the article. When someone is pitching to me, I want to know they can write the piece, so it's important to convey that ability. While personal experience is helpful, I want to see evidence that the person can report and write, and that they know how to get hold of and quote experts.

Ninety-nine percent of the queries I get are inappropriate. For a custom publication like *ATA World*, it's important to understand that there's a client — in this case the ATA — as well as the editor and the end user. Get to know the organization, which you can do by visiting the Web site. Recognize that if you want to write a piece profiling a competing organization, we're not going to run that. And because we're a magazine about taekwondo, we don't want articles about cage fighting, and we don't want articles about kung fu. Our audience includes kids, and a lot of it is about building life skills.

West
(Los Angeles Times Magazine)

When you think of pitching profiles, you probably envision sitting across the table from some hunky actor or powerful politician, scribbling away as your subject spouts *bon mots*. But what about that lady who volunteers at the school cross walk? Or the guy who runs the little model train store on Main Street? As you'll see from this query, everybody has a story — and if you can highlight their character with a strong voice, you've got a sure winner.

Wrapped In The Arms Of The Blues

Our story in an absurdist nutshell: two years ago a middle-aged black woman named Margaret Ann Long Dolan, a/k/a Ann the Raven,* was handling announcing chores at a Los Angeles-area blues festival. She introduced her old friend, blues legend Etta James, who needed an electric scooter chair to make it up onto the stage. On her way back to the wings Ann tripped over the ramp hastily installed for Miss James, landed on her knee and tore her cartilage. She has no health insurance, so she still limps.

Ann the Raven is the blues incarnate. Unlike most talented people who arrive in Los Angeles, then achieve artistic success, then loftily declare that they're remaining true to their artistic principles, Ann — the most knowledgeable and hypnotically entertaining practitioner of her niche art form in Southern California—would love to sell out. The only problem is that nobody's buying.

In the meantime she does what she does best, and does it hypnotically well. Listeners to her two weekly programs (Sundays 8 p.m. to midnight and Mondays 9 to midnight) on public radio station KCSN are likely to hear a splendid set of recordings by such artists as James, B.B. King, John Lee Hooker, Stevie Ray Vaughn, and perhaps Janis Joplin or Billie Holliday. Or maybe her signature song, "Blues In The City," by Larry McCray. Then Ann cuts in:

"This is Ann the Raven, in case you just tuned in, darlin', and I'm dishing out the blues for you this Sunday night. This is a holiday weekend, yeah! And for you people who work — hey! A long weekend. You should be out there playing, having fun. I'm thinking about the things I used to do all those Sunday nights — before I got fat, you know. I used to be one wild chick! And I was thinking: I want that back! I gotta get rid of this fat! [choked sound from deep in her throat that might be laughing, might be crying]

"Life in the big city hasn't been pretty for the Raven, but she's hangin' in there. She's doin' the best she can. She's gonna make you happy tonight, though. I know I will. Because I'm gonna try. Earlier of course you heard Larry McCray with 'Blues In The City,' — and honey, let me tell you that the Raven's got blues in the city. L.A.'s a city to have blues in. Let me tell you: I've no money, fat, black, hey — what can I say? Broke, no career, no life, love — oh, I need love so bad!

"Hey, my city is not pretty, I can tell you that. But I'm gonna hang in there 'till it gets better."

Or maybe more to the point, on a special "love-themed" Valentine's Day blues show:

"I don't know, guys, about playing all this 'love' music tonight. It's just not doing it for me. It's just not doing it. I want to feel the blues. I guess I'm not happy unless I'm unhappy [approximately same choked sound as above]. I just can't figure it out. I need to hear something tough. But I gotta remind myself that it is other people out there who're in love and I gotta play it for the lovers. So darlin', I'm going to stick with it for a while. I myself, I admit that I — I keep hoping that one day I'll have someone who I'll feel strong about. Feel good about. I don't know. I can't give up. I ain't gonna give up. I can't give up on love."

Quite an act, you say? Except it isn't. Margaret Ann Long Dolan, who of course gets no money from KCSN, the low-to-medium power (on a good day) radio station at Cal State Northridge, hasn't had a real job for over a year. She scrapes up whatever income she can by babysitting and doing other off-the-books chores and shares the rent for her tiny Pasadena apartment with her roommate, a white Belgian guy she can barely understand. She drives a 1984 Mustang convertible with a duct-tape collage top, three bald tires and one undersized spare. She sometimes has to borrow gas money to get to the station. She is indeed overweight; she huffs and puffs as she pulls her wheeled suitcase filled with her personal collection of blues CDs into KCSN's tiny studio, located in the bottom left hand corner of a dormitory building.

How she got into this fix is a blues CD in itself. She was born and raised in Stillwater, Oklahoma, where her mother, a blues fanatic, force-fed her the canon. Sufficiently bummed by her surroundings, she headed west in her early 20s. Segue to an interesting five-year marriage, her first and so far her last, to an Irishman in Sausalito. Messy divorce over, she moved down to L.A. and stumbled into a good administrative assistant job at Pasadena City College, where she enrolled part time and — most importantly — got her own blues show on KPCC. Ann the Raven had a long-running show on this perennial competitor to public radio's Alpha L.A. station, KCRW, for fifteen years. She attracted thousands of steady listeners and became a fixture on L.A.'s small-but-persistent blues performance scene. During those fairly happy years she got her degree at PCC, transferred her credits to USC, and got her B.A. — just in time to watch KPCC get acquired by Minnesota Public Radio and transmuted into an all-talk format.

And oh, yeah: Did I mention that Ann's USC degree is in Humanities?

Good morning, heartache. She sent her resume to KKJZ, the popular blues-and-jazz station at Long Beach State, and discovered that "somebody there definitely doesn't like me." She caught on at KCSN, if not in the job market, and now has hundreds of fans in Germany via the Internet. Also, several half-formed schemes to become a professional child custody mediator; open a combination coffee bar/blues performance space; get a job as a DJ in Europe, etc. She's also very open to working in the jazz, rock or even country radio formats: but her bluesy job history, she says, keeps her behind the eight ball in those arenas, alas.

In the short time I've spent with her I've definitely detected a strain of masochism and/or self-destruction: for instance, in directing me to our first meeting she told me that Cal State Northridge, which I'd never before been to, is at the corner of "Lesson and Zephyr." It's actually at Lassen and Zelzah. She got caught in traffic and was a half an hour late to our interview.

And yet.

If Ann was the just the Voice of Depression in Los Angeles she would be unlistenable. She's far from that. She's a big fundraiser during the station's fund drives; as she sits and does her show she gets many calls from listeners; many of them lonely and lovelorn Angelos who turn to her for moral support. She gives it to them; she's also beloved by her public radio co-workers and by this country's under-recognized and hard-working corps of blues musicians—many of whom she's extensively interviewed and whose tape-recorded recollections disappeared forever, big surprise, when Ann's storage shed was burgled recently.

My guesstimate is that Ann's about 35 percent victim, 35 percent survivor, and a sneaky 15 percent cockeyed optimism.

That raises the chicken-and-egg question: does Ann play the blues so well because she's so blue, or is she blue because she plays the blues so well? Either way, she seems to make it back to the studio every week. How? Why? Those are the journo-existential matters I plan to explore in this piece.

And if you don't give me the assignment, I just don't know what I'll do.

Best,
Andy

*Ann won't reveal the genesis of her nickname, which she says is "mortifying." I have a good idea how she got it, and she's right.

The Writer: Andy Meisler

I was listening to the radio and heard this woman on a little public radio station that not a lot of people listen to. I thought, "This has got to be an act!" I kept listening to her and then I called her up and asked to meet her; I just said, "I write a lot for the *L.A. Times Magazine* and I'd love to pitch a story idea about you. Can I come up there and meet you?" Obviously that won't work if it's, say, Condoleezza Rice, but it worked in this case. I don't tend to do stories about people you've already heard about, and that gives me an advantage. People like to talk about themselves — especially people who haven't had articles written about them already. So I met her and it wasn't an act. She really has the blues!

You want to get the editor's attention ASAP. The danger there is resorting to cheap tricks. I think the top of this query is a bit snarky. As I kept writing I worried whether it was too snarky and I would be perceived as putting down this person, which I certainly didn't want to do. Lower down in the query I made it plain that I think this woman is fascinating and that I'm not riffing on her poverty or her situation. I'm saying how unfair it is that this woman is caught in a conundrum.

The query didn't seem long to me; a lot of it was copying down her rap. I put the information in a triangular shape [with the most important information first] so the editor can read as much as he wants. The most important part is the beginning; if I can keep him reading, he'll be interested in assigning the story.

My ending is playfully "bluesy." One of the reasons this query worked is that I have a long and wonderful relationship with the editor. He knows that I can deliver. I don't know if this ending would have worked otherwise.

The most important thing you need to convey to an editor is that you want to do this story, not that you want to fill some perceived hole in the magazine. Obviously you see what sections the magazine has and what articles they have in each section, but you want to show that this is a story you really want to do instead of saying, "This will fill a hole in your magazine." Don't try to sound like the Writer's Guide — let it all hang out.

And for God's sake — when I was an editor, the worst thing was seeing stationery that says what writer's association the writer belongs to. No real writer puts "Travel Writers of Montana" on their letterhead. It just looks amateurish, like you're the kind of person who goes to writers' conferences a lot but doesn't do much writing for money. I can't tell you how many letterheads we got that had little doodles of guys or gals sitting under palm trees with typewriters. Next!

The Editor: Martin J. Smith, Senior Editor

This pitch was pretty irresistible ... and I have no idea who this woman is. There may be 500 people who listen to her, and it doesn't matter because she's so compelling that you're immediately engaged. Andy is a storyteller. The voice was the preeminent thing here, and Andy's got a knack for that. He takes a different eye to things.

Voice involves unlearning a lot of what you learned in journalism school. You've done all the research — now shove that pile of notes aside and tell me a story. Don't fall into the formulaic quote/attribution set-up. Learn how to set scenes, learn how to develop characters in a way that I'm immediately engaged and I care what happens to them. This isn't about efficiently conveying information; it's about sucking me into somebody's life and helping me understand something important.

I could tell Andy put a lot of thought into the query, and it's perfect. The ending is so good, I can tell you what the last line is from memory. I just thought, "Yeah, this is something he'll knock out of the park." He seemed to understand the blues experience.

I think that normally, one page is plenty to sketch out an idea. If the idea is something we're interested in, we'll have a conversation to flesh out the idea. But in that initial pitch, you need to have voice. I need to know you're not going to make a few phone calls and do a few interviews and write it up. I need to know why this is an important story to tell.

If the object of a story is to "show not tell," the object of the pitch is to tell. Connect the dots and tell me why our readers would care about this. Don't just show it and expect me to connect the dots. Explain to me, "This is important because ...."

The pitch should be timely, and make it very clear why the story is important at this point in time. More often than not I get ideas that lack that component. The writer will say, "This is the 50th anniversary of such-and-such." So what? Last year was the 49th anniversary of such-and-such. If it's important now because there's legislation that's coming up for a vote in June, tell me that. We're a news magazine.

Writer Bios

Karen Ansel is a registered dietitian and freelance writer in Long Island, NY. Her work has appeared in *Fitness, Shape, Woman's Day, Family Circle, Cooking Light* and *Marie Claire.*

Jena Ball has been writing professionally for over 20 years now. Her work includes everything from syndicated columns and book reviews to travel/adventure pieces and celebrity profiles. She has written for a wide range of publications including *Backpacker, House Beautiful, Mother Earth News, E,* and *The Japan Times.*

Playboy writer **Damon Brown** is the author of *The Pocket Idiot's Guide to the iPod.* He has a Masters in Magazine Publishing from Northwestern University's Medill School of Journalism. Read his writing at www.damonbrown.net.

Beverly Burmeier is a Texas-based writer specializing in health and nutrition, lifestyle, travel, gardening, and parenting. Her articles have appeared in *Oxygen, Woman's Day, American Profile, The History Channel Magazine, E/The Environmental Magazine, Ladies' Home Journal,* and a variety of other national publications.

Rick Chillot escaped a full-time office job at a national magazine about eight years ago to work from home as a freelance writer and editor. Some of the topics he's covered in that time include cardiovascular disease, impotence, Peru, abs, bicycle mechanics, cancer, grilling, vampires and the mysteries of the human heart. He's authored one novella, several chapters in various books, one nonfiction book on pain relief, a handful of short stories about the forces of darkness and a kajillion nonfiction magazine and web articles. He lives in rural Pennsylvania where he is occasionally sighted outside his house and enjoys cycling, volunteering at the local NPR station and learning to play the guitar.

Ren Collins is a musician and writer who lives in Brooklyn, NY with her fiance, Alex and their cat, Woodstock.

Query Letters that Rock

Kathryn Cordova has written science and feature articles for *Water Pollution Control Journal, Water & Wastes Engineering, Irrigation Age, Old Mill News, New Mexico Magazine, Tradicion Revista* (ghost writing), various farm and gardening magazines, *Southwest Restaurateur,* and *El Restaurante Mexicano.* She's also the editor of the New Mexico Branch monthly newsletter of the International Foodservice Executives Association.

Dalia Fahmy has worked as a reporter and television producer for more than a decade, with stints in Cairo, Singapore, Brussels and Frankfurt. Currently based in New York, she writes about business, travel and house and home. She is the author of Frommer's online Egypt travel guide, and her articles have appeared in newspapers and magazines such as *The New York Times, Financial Times, New York Post, The Miami Herald,* and *National Geographic Traveler.*

Dalia began her career as a wire service correspondent in Frankfurt, where she covered European economic affairs for Knight-Ridder Financial News. She later moved to New York to write about Latin American finance for Bridge News, eventually supervising a large team of reporters and directing coverage of global emerging market crises. As a senior segment producer at CNBC television she worked on the top-rated program *Squawk Box,* and has also helped produce lifestyle features for Germany's Spiegel-TV.

Jacquelyn B. Fletcher is a freelance writer whose book *A Career Girl's Guide to Becoming a Stepmom* is forthcoming from HarperCollins in January 2007. She writes and edits for various magazines and teaches at the Loft Literary Center in Minneapolis.

Susan T. Lennon lives in Rocky Hill, CT with her husband and their two dogs and cat. Her credits include *Newsweek's* "My Turn," *The Washington Post* "Styles" section, *USA Weekend Magazine, Health, Prevention, ATA World, The AKC Gazette,* and others. Visit her website: www.susanlennon.com

Andy Meisler is a writer and editor. He is the co-author of *The Secret Life of Cyndy Garvey* with Cynthia Garvey and *I Am Roe: My Life,*

Roe v. Wade and Freedom of Choice with Norma McCorvey. He writes frequently for *The New York Times,* the *Los Angeles Times Magazine* and several other national publications. He lives in Los Angeles with his wife Emily.

Lori B. Murray has been working as a freelance writer since 1995. She has written numerous magazine and newspaper articles, with credits that include *Woman's Day, Family Fun, Ohio Magazine* and *American Profile.* She teaches writing at Columbus State Community College in Columbus, Ohio, where she lives with her husband and three children.

After graduating from Middlebury College in 2001, **Devon O'Neil** took a job as a counter-terrorism analyst in Washington, D.C. He lasted one year, then moved to Breckenridge, CO, where he works as the sports editor of the *Summit Daily News.* He has won state awards for event, column and feature writing. Reach him at devononeil@hotmail.com.

Amy Paturel provides health communication services to a variety of clients, from general interest magazines to medical e-zines. Her work frequently appears in such publications as *Cooking Light, Men's Health, Self, SHAPE, Better Homes and Gardens,* and *Marie Claire.* Amy is a columnist for AOL's Diet and Fitness Channels and a member of the American Society of Journalists and Authors (ASJA).

Ellise Pierce is a freelance writer who divides her time between Dallas and Paris. She has written for *Newsweek, People, Jane, Redbook, Cooking Light, Texas Monthly, American Way, Delta Sky,* and *Northwest Airlines' Hemispheres.*

Paul Raffaele is a freelance writer who specializes in stories from remote places. His work has appeared in *Smithsonian, Parade, Reader's Digest* and other publications.

Cynthia Ramnarace is a writer based in Brooklyn, N.Y. After nearly 10 years in newspapers, she started freelancing for magazines in 2005. Health writing and features are her specialty. She may be reached through her Web site, www.cynthiaramnarace.com.

For more than 25 years **Jim Robbins** has written about environmental and political issues from his home in Helena, Montana, with an emphasis on the changing American West. He was born in Niagara Falls, New York, and came to Montana in 1976 to live in a part of the world where nature had not been overwhelmed by civilization. Since 1980 he has been a regular contributor to *The New York Times*, writing about everything from the Unabomber to the Freeman, wildfires, threats to national parks — especially Yellowstone — wolverines, grizzly bears and wolves. He contributes to the *Los Angeles Times Magazine, Smithsonian, Audubon* and has appeared as an analyst on ABC's *Nightline* and NPR's *All Things Considered* and *Morning Edition*. He has traveled throughout the world, from South America to Asia and Europe on assignment for various magazines and newspapers. Though his specialty is environment and natural science, he has written extensively about the human central nervous system, especially Attention Deficit Disorder, anxiety and depression. He's the author of two books, *Last Refuge: Environmental Showdown in the American West* and *A Symphony in the Brain: The Evolution of the New Brainwave Biofeedback*. A third book, *The Open-Focus Brain: Using the Power of Attention to Heal Mind and Body*, is due out in early 2007.

Julia Rosien is a former senior editor at *ePregnancy Magazine*. Her freelance credits include publications such as *The Boston Globe, Wedding Style, Spirituality & Health, The Christian Science Monitor* and the *American Bar Association Journal*.

Jebra Turner has been a full-time freelancer for a decade, writing about career and business issues for corporations and magazines. Previous to that she was human resources manager at a spin-off of the high-tech giant, Tektronix. She lives in Portland, Oregon where it's often rainy, gray, and overcast — perfect writing weather!

Melody Warnick, a freelancer from Ames, Iowa, writes for *Better Homes and Gardens, Parenting, American Baby*, and *American Profile* and covers health, parenting, relationships and home topics, among others. You can read more about Melody and her work at www.melody-warnick.com.

Alison Stein Wellner is a contributing editor at *Inc.*, and writes for publications ranging from *American Archaeology* to the *Washington Post*, with stops in between at *Glamour, Mother Jones,* and *Reason,* among other magazines and newspapers. Check out her website at www.wellner.biz.

Tim Wendel is the author of five books, including *Castro's Curveball: A Novel.* His articles have appeared in *Esquire, GQ, The New York Times, The Washington Post, The Los Angeles Times, National Geographic Traveler* and *USA Weekend.* He teaches writing at Johns Hopkins University.

Our Acknowledgements

First, a big thanks to our publisher and editor, Ed Avis. Ed and his team of magic gnomes at Marion Street Press make the whole process of writing and editing easy and enjoyable for us. A special thanks for Anne Locascio for another rocking cover design!

A big thanks goes to the writers who graciously agreed to share their outstanding query letters with thousands of readers, and spent hours patiently answering our nosy questions: Teri Cettina, Devon O'Neil, Melody Warnick, Alison Stein Wellner, Damon Brown, Ren Collins, Beverly Burmeier, Jena Ball, Lori Murray, Tim Wendel, Andy Meisler, Rick Chillot, Karen Ansel, Jim Robbins, Cynthia Ramnarace, Julia Rosien, Jebra Turner, Jeannette Hurt, Paul Raffaele, Kathryn Cordova, Susan Lennon, Ellise Pierce, Dalia Fahmy, Amy Paturel, and Jacqueline Fletcher.

A round of applause for the editors who commented on those query letters, often spending much more time than we'd originally allocated to the project, and who gave us quotes for the FAQ: Sarah Smith, Cara McDonald, Larry Kanter, Dennis McCafferty, Lisa Hannam, Leah Flickinger, Christine Porretta, Carey Rossi, Leah McLaughlin, Martin J. Smith, Neely Harris, Eric Lucas, Ken Budd, Tim Clancy, Karen Axelton, Richard McVey, Kristin Godsey, Jennifer Lawler, Kathleen Furore, Dobby Gibson and Ron Kovach.

Our biggest thanks goes to the readers of our first and second editions of *The Renegade Writer*, who've been nothing but supportive of us. You guys don't know how proud you make us, out there breaking rules left and right.

Diana's Acknowledgements:

A special thanks to Jenna Schnuer, Gwen Moran, Deb Carpenter, and Monica Bhide, who answered my questions.

More thanks to the students I've taught in my magazine writing class over the past three years at Chelmsford (MA) Community Education and Middlesex Community College in Bedford, MA. Many of the questions they asked ended up in this book, the answers for which were made more eloquent by the awesome writing and editing skills of my co-author …

Linda Formichelli! The best co-author a girl could ask for. I'll sip tea with you anytime!

And lastly, a big thanks to my husband and son. I love you both.

Linda's Acknowledgements

I'd like to thank my husband W. Eric Martin, who is a total hunk o' hotness and a great writer to boot. Also thanks to my mom and dad, who buy all my books even though I would totally give them free copies.

Thanks to all the students of my e-course, who have asked many of the questions in the Frequently Asked Questions section of this book. May you land many lucrative assignments.

And a special thanks to my co-author Diana Burrell. I lift my cup of tea to you, o awesome one!

Index